Pieced Border Collection™

Designs by
Denyse Saint Arroman

Edited by
Sandra L. Hatch

HOUSE of
WHITE
BIRCHES
PUBLISHERS
SINCE 1947

Pieced Border Collection

Editor: Sandra L. Hatch
Copy Editor: Cathy Reef
Product Coordinator: Jeanne Stauffer
Editorial Director: Vivian Rothe

Production Manager: Vicki Macy
Creative Coordinator: Shaun Venish
Technical Artist: Connie Rand
Production Artist: Brenda Gallmeyer
Production Coordinator: Sandra Ridgway Beres
Production Assistant: Cheryl Lynch

Publishers: Carl H. Muselman, Arthur K. Muselman
Chief Executive Officer: John Robinson
Marketing Director: Scott Moss

Printed in the United States of America
First Printing: 1996
Library of Congress Number: 95-81674
ISBN: 882138-13-9

Pieced Borders
Add the Finishing Touch

Starting in 1982 Eula Long's Royal Stars of the States patterns began to appear in *Quilt World*. For over six years, one or two designs were printed in every issue.

During that time Dolores Yoder from Paris, Texas, collected the patterns and made all 50 quilts. Because of their popularity, the patterns were printed together as a collection showing Dolores' quilts as examples of how the patterns could be interpreted in color.

At the same time, Denyse Saint Arroman from France was collecting the patterns and making her versions of the quilts.

Most of the original patterns did not include border designs. Like Dolores, Denyse added her own borders. Over time, she designed borders for each Royal Star quilt. She wrote to *Quilt World* to share some of her designs. Through that correspondence an idea was formed to share Denyse's border designs in a book for others who liked the Royal Star patterns as well as for quilters who like to add pieced borders to their quilts.

Pieced Border Collection is the result of that idea. It is not possible to show photographs of Denyse's actual quilts because she sold every one. Finding and transporting them to the United States for photography became too much of a problem.

Even though all of the patterns in this book were designed specifically for one of the Royal Stars quilts, each design can be used on other quilts as well. Our general instructions guide you in using these designs on quilts of other sizes and give you hints for making your quilt center and chosen border fit each other.

A good border reflects some of the design principles of the center design. It also uses colors found in the center design. Yardage figures are not given in a list; rather they are given with each template, giving you the option of choosing any color combination. You may then determine how much fabric you need for each color.

To show you how beautiful the border designs can look when added to a quilt center, we used drawings of the original Royal Stars quilts. This by no means limits any of the borders' use. They can be used on any quilt, if the design shapes complement the quilt center.

Quilts without borders are like a cake without frosting. The cake might taste good without the frosting, but with frosting it tastes better and looks more appetizing. A border on a quilt doesn't make it any warmer, but it does frame the center design and adds much more than size to the finished quilt.

Consider adding a pieced border to your next quilt. Choose a design from this book that will enhance the design of your quilt center. Plan the colors on the border to include those used in the center of the quilt to confine the design and add emphasis to the center.

Remember the concepts of good design when choosing a border design. Consider scale and proportion. A good border design does not overwhelm the quilt center design. Repeat design elements, fabrics and colors for continuity.

Have fun combining a pieced border with your quilt center. When you are finished you won't believe the difference the extra effort and time will make in your finished quilt.

Note: Should you decide you like the quilt center shown with each border design, ordering information is given for the Royal Stars of the States *book on Page 159.*

Pieced Border Collection

Pieced Borders

General Instructions

All 50 of the border designs in this book are pieced. Some have many small pieces with very sharp angles making them difficult to piece; others have larger pieces and softer angles and are easy to piece.

Following are instructions for making templates, hand or machine piecing, changing sizes and how to use the patterns given. General instructions for finishing the pieced tops into quilts are also included. Please note that this is a design book, not a method book. It is assumed that the reader has quilting knowledge and/or has other books from which to learn these techniques.

Leaf through the pages of this book and choose several border designs you especially like that will enhance your quilt. Analyze the shapes in each design to determine which border includes similar shapes as those used in your quilt center.

Yardage Needed

Note that our color drawings show border designs which are color coordinated with the colors used in the quilt center. The colors used in each piece are not limited to the combinations used. For this reason, we have supplied templates with yardage for each piece.

To determine total yardage needed, choose colors for each piece. It might help to color in the unfilled piecing diagrams. If several pieces use the same color, total the yardage needed for each piece to find how much fabric you need.

For example, in the Wisconsin border (Page 154), piece 2 is shown in the color drawing in two colors. Template 2 lists fabric needed at 1 1/2 yards total. If piece 2 is cut from two different fabrics, you would need 3/4 yard of each. If you decide to use five fabrics, you would need 1/3 yard each.

If you cut piece 1 from more than one fabric, divide the total needed by the number of colors you want to use to determine the amount needed of each color.

The corner units are usually cut from the same color as other pieces in the border. Because you only need a few of these pieces, separate yardage is not given, but the templates tell you to use the same fabric as another piece. You may change the color completely or use the same color as a different piece.

If we had given a list of fabrics to buy, it would have included the colors shown in the color drawings and would not have been as helpful to you if you want to change colors. We hope this listing of fabrics needed for each template will be helpful.

If you are planning a whole quilt, add the border yardage amounts to the colors needed for the pieced center to guarantee that you will have enough fabric to use the pieced center colors in the borders.

Making the Border Fit Your Quilt

Most of the border patterns were designed to fit quilts with square centers: 72" x 72", 75" x 75" and 78" x 78". Sometimes plain border strips had to be added to the original quilt center to make it the right size to be divisible by the border unit size.

Take Alabama, for example. The border unit for that quilt is 6" along the inside edge of each unit. The finished quilt center was 75" x 75" which is not evenly divisible by six. There are two 3" No. 2 pieces at the base of each unit. If you add 3" to

the center to make a 78" x 78" center, you can divide that number evenly by 6 to get 13 units.

If the quilt center needs 3" all around to make it 78" square, a 1 1/2" (finished size) border strip should be added to each side. That was simple.

What if your quilt center is not a square but a rectangle? You may have to add different width border strips to the top and bottom than to the sides to make the border units work.

Using the same border unit, let's pretend your quilt center finishes at 66" x 84". No, that's too easy; 66 divided by six equals 11 and 84 divided by six equals 14! You won't need to add anything except 11 border units on two sides and 14 on the other two sides! Try 67" x 85". Now, that's a bit harder. You don't get an even number when you divide six into 67 or into 85. What do we need to add to 67 to make it work? When you divided, you had 11 with one left over. Add five to that one to make six and try 72. Yes, that's 12—so 12 units will fit on that side if you add 5" all around. To add 5" you need 2 1/2" strips on each side of the quilt center.

Don't forget to add a seam allowance to all measurements before cutting the border strips. A 2 1/2"-wide finished strip should be cut 3" wide.

What about 85? Dividing six into 85 equals 14 with one left over, so five works on that side as well. We didn't mean for it to work out that way. How about trying 86"? Now you have 14 with two left over. You will need 4" borders on that side to make an even 15 units on that side. Because the border strips are different widths, you cannot miter the corners when the strips are added to the quilt center. Butt them as shown in Figure 1.

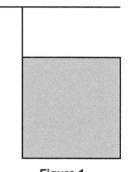

Figure 1
Butted borders at corners are necessary when border strips are different widths.

It is simple to make these borders fit any quilt center. By adding strips to the center or by adding or taking away units, you can make your quilt almost any size you want.

Making Templates

The patterns given in this book are actual size; they do not include a 1/4" seam allowance. When making templates for hand piecing, accurately trace the shape onto template material. Cut out the shape on the marked line to create a template.

If you prefer templates with a 1/4" seam allowance already added for machine piecing, after transferring the shape to the template material, add a 1/4" seam allowance all around.

Transfer the grain-line arrows and cutting information to the templates.

Cutting Fabric

Fabric may be prewashed if desired. If you choose not to prewash your fabrics, test them to be sure they are colorfast. Wet a sample of each fabric and stack it against the other fabrics to see if color transfers from darker fabrics to lighter fabrics. If they do, do not use the offending fabric in your quilt.

Iron the fabric to remove wrinkles. Lay it out on a flat surface right side down. Use a sharp No. 2 lead pencil or other sharp washable marking tool to trace shape onto fabric, using grain lines on templates as guides for placement.

If your templates do not have the 1/4" seam allowance added, leave 1/2" between pieces when marking on fabric as shown in Figure 2.

To reverse a piece, turn the template over with writing on the back. Space pieces as close together as possible as shown in Figure 3.

marking tool to draw lines around your pieces. This extra step marks an exact 1/4" which makes machine piecing easy, but is not necessary for hand piecing. Hand piecing is recommended for many of the more complicated designs.

Store all cut pieces in sealable plastic bags with the template. The pieces of some of the border designs are very similar in size and shape, and it would be very easy to mix them up later when piecing.

When all fabric pieces are cut, you are ready to sew.

Sewing Pieces Together

Each border pattern has figure drawings to help you determine the easiest way to piece each unit. There are no written instructions telling you to sew piece 1 to 2 and so on. Use the drawings as guides for piecing the units.

If you are an experienced sewer and will be piecing by machine, you may prefer to sew all like units using chain piecing as shown in Figure 4. In this method you might sew all 1 and 2 pieces together and then all 3 and 4 pieces, etc., before piecing them in units.

For hand piecers, it is more satisfying to piece one unit at a time. As you finish the units, you can see your design take shape.

When hand-piecing, begin stitching at the end of the marked seam line, not at the end of the piece, as shown in Figure 5. Start sewing with a knotted thread right at the point. Take a small running stitch and then a backstitch to secure the seam.

Continue sewing a running stitch to the end of the seam at the other end of the piece and repeat backstitching. Make a knot through the loop in the backstitch before pulling thread taut and cutting away (Figure 6).

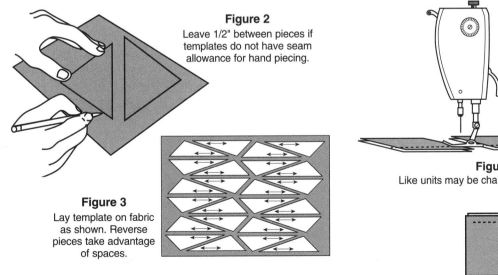

Figure 2
Leave 1/2" between pieces if templates do not have seam allowance for hand piecing.

Figure 3
Lay template on fabric as shown. Reverse pieces take advantage of spaces.

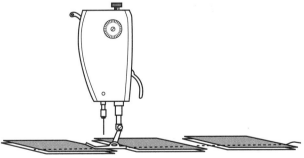

Figure 4
Like units may be chain-pieced by machine.

Figure 5
For hand piecing, start sewing at the beginning of the seam, not the end of the piece.

You may layer the fabrics for cutting to save time. Pin layers together to keep flat when cutting.

After marking pieces onto fabric, cut out, leaving 1/4" on each side. If you are not secure eyeballing the 1/4", use a 1/4"

Figure 6
Make a loop in the backstitch to make
a knot at the end of the seam.

When machine-piecing, most seams can be sewn from one edge of the piece to the other. If one piece is set into another, begin and end as for hand piecing as shown in Figure 7.

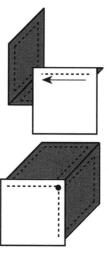

Figure 7
Set-in seams are stitched the same for
both hand and machine piecing.

About the Designer

Denyse Saint Arroman is a French designer with a long history of needlework accomplishments. She states that she has always been a craft person with interest in embroidery, tapestry, macramé, sewing, etc.

In 1977 she joined her husband, a French liaison officer, at the Field Artillery School in Fort Sill, Okla.

It was at Fort Sill that Denyse discovered quilting. She joined a group of officers' wives with the purpose of improving her English, not to learn to quilt.

She became fascinated with the endless possibilities quilting offered and has been quilting ever since. She stopped counting the number of quilts she has made when she reached 100.

Denyse likes to try all techniques. Her favorite type is the crazy quilt. She finds the wonderful intricacy of embroidery combined with adding beads can create a contemporary look.

Denyse's college education in history combines with her love of needlework to create a history of her own. She is the author of several quilting books in her home country, France, and has been honored with many awards.

She was an international winner in the Memories of Childhood contest, won first prize with Les Bouquets in a contest organized by the French Guild, second prize for Le Bicentenaire organized by the same group, third prize in Quilt UK and a merit award in the National Championship in England.

Denyse's quilts have traveled to many distinguished exhibitions including the Memories of Childhood, a traveling U.S. exhibition from 1988–1991, at the Houston International Quilt Festival in 1989, Quilt Europa, 1990–92 and 1994, a touring exhibition in Japan in 1994 and other exhibitions too numerous to mention.

In spite of all her accomplishments and honors, Denyse says from time to time she still likes to work with traditional patterns. Creating her own border and quilting designs to accompany these designs gives her the impetus to continue the quilting and designing she loves.

When hand-piecing units, finger-press seams. When each unit is complete, iron to make crisp seam joints. Check the back for neatness and trim any threads.

When machine piecing, press seams before joining with other units; since seams will be sewn into other seams, they cannot be pressed flat after being stitched over.

Joining Units

When the correct number of units have been completed, join them together in rows for each side. It helps to press finished and joined units before sewing to the quilt center.

Remeasure the quilt center and the pieced border strips to be sure the strips will fit. Adjust border strips or quilt center if necessary.

Piece corner units referring to the figure drawings. Sew a pieced border strip to two opposite sides. Sew a corner unit to each end of the remaining two border strips before sewing to quilt center. Press the entire quilt top before preparing to quilt.

Finishing

This book does not include any quilting designs. There are many sources for beautiful quilt patterns available including purchased plastic quilting templates.

Find the perfect quilting design to fill in the large unpieced areas of your quilt center. Mark the chosen design on the finished quilt top using a water-erasable marker or pencil.

Some quilt designs are enhanced if pieces are quilted in the ditch of the seams or 1/4" away from seams. This is a personal choice. Large open areas should be filled with a pretty design.

Backing fabric should be of the same fiber content as the quilt top and should not show through to the top. Do not use a dark backing with a light-colored top; the dark color will shadow through to the lighter fabrics.

Prepare a backing piece to fit your quilt top. Add 4" to the quilt top size all around and prepare the backing piece that size. You may seam pieces in several ways as shown in Figure 8.

Fold and press the backing to mark centers. Purchase a batting at least 4" larger than your quilt size.

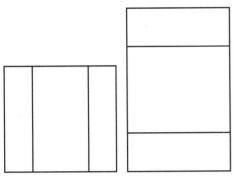

Figure 8
Backings may be pieced as shown.

Lay the backing right side down on a large flat surface. Tape or clamp to secure. Flatten out the batting and center on the backing. Trim to backing size if it is too large. Tape or clamp it in place as well.

Fold and crease your quilt top to mark centers. Match these crease lines up with the lines on the backing piece. Pin in place from the center to the outside. Remove tape or clamps at this time, if desired.

Using a long unknotted piece of light-colored thread and a long large needle, start making large basting stitches from the center of your quilt to the outside. Continue basting in this manner every 4" until quilt top is completely basted.

Quilt on marked lines and elsewhere as desired. Make small even stitches, sink your knots at the beginning and end and check the back often. There should be no lumps or creases and stitches should be as neat on the back as on the front.

When quilting is complete, trim edges even. Choose a purchased binding, or make your own from fabric strips matching the fabrics in your quilt. Bias binding is the most durable to use on an heirloom quilt as the edges get a lot of wear.

Strips for bias binding are cut across the diagonal of the fabric and joined to make one long continuous strip. To make an even more durable edge, fold the binding strips in half right sides out to make a double layer.

Adding an interesting and intricate border to your pieced center is satisfying and well worth the extra time and effort; it adds so much to the finished quilt. If you have been adding plain strips to all of your quilt tops as a border finish, try using one of the designs from this book on your next quilt and see the difference.

Designer's Note

In 1982 *Quilt World* magazine started printing the Royal Stars of the States pattern series. I found the designs to be spectacular, exciting and fast to piece.

When my daughter asked me to make a quilt for her bed, I decided to try one of the Royal Stars—I chose South Carolina. It took me one week to complete the quilt.

At that time my daughter wanted everything around her to be purple. She was not the tidiest teen-ager in the world. I didn't want to spend months making a fine quilt which would be ruined or discarded in a short time. (This is always my policy when making quilts for children!)

The quilt turned out quite well and a picture of it was published in *Elle* to illustrate the advertisement of a newly opened quilt shop.

Still, I was not completely satisfied; I thought the quilt lacked something to balance the central design and frame the quilt. I always encourage my students to design their own borders and quilting patterns. I hate when they choose any design just because it is the one available.

I feel that a border design must echo and enhance the central design. It is not something you add just to give the quilt the right size or because you have been taught that a quilt must have a border.

I couldn't do less than to give the example and to put into practice what I teach. That was my reason for designing borders for the other quilts I made using the Royal Stars as the center design.

I made many of the Royal Stars of the States designs into quilts. I designed a border for each one. As time went by, I found it exciting to design a border to match every design. The results are in this book.

I would like to thank designer Eula Long for those Royal Stars of the States patterns. The time I have spent working with them and these border designs has been happy.

—*Denyse Saint Arroman*

Alabama Pieced Border

The diamond shape used in this border design is repeated from the shape used in the quilt's center. Use this border pattern on any star quilt center as the perfect edge finish.

Border Unit: 7" wide
Pieced Triangle Base: 6" wide—13 per side

Border is shown with the star pattern for Royal Star of Alabama. The pattern for the star is available in *Royal Stars of the States*, also published by House of White Birches. See ordering information on Page 159.

Alabama Pieced Border
Placement Diagram
Star Center 75" x 75"
Add 1 1/2" borders—78" x 78"
With Borders 92" x 92"
With 1 1/2" Outside Borders 95" x 95"

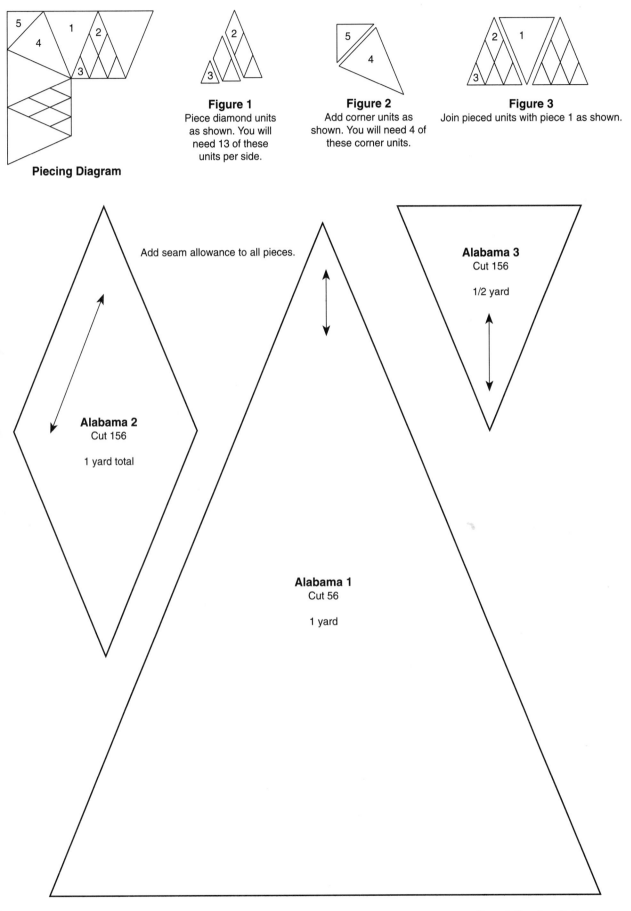

Piecing Diagram

Figure 1
Piece diamond units as shown. You will need 13 of these units per side.

Figure 2
Add corner units as shown. You will need 4 of these corner units.

Figure 3
Join pieced units with piece 1 as shown.

Add seam allowance to all pieces.

Alabama 2
Cut 156

1 yard total

Alabama 3
Cut 156

1/2 yard

Alabama 1
Cut 56

1 yard

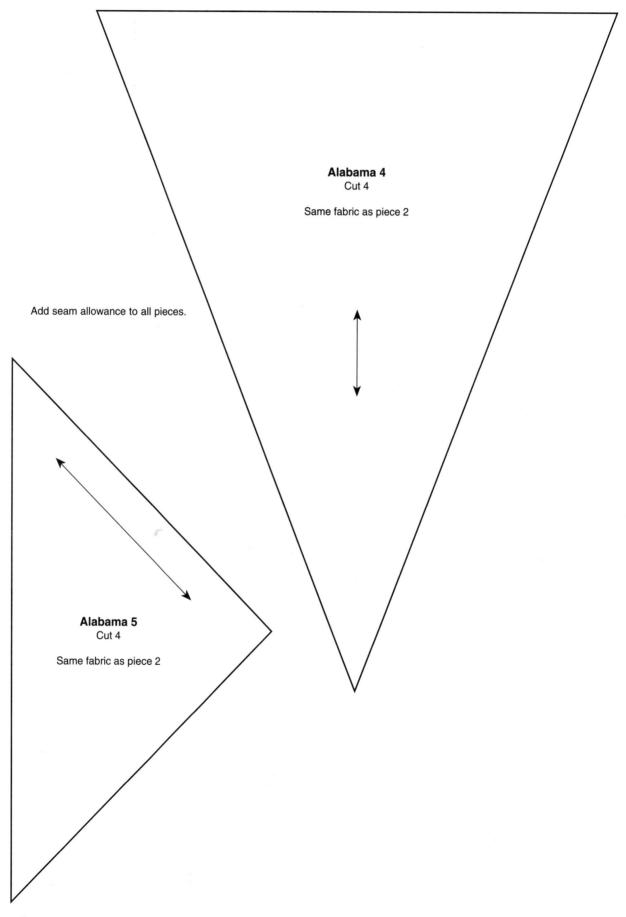

Alabama 4
Cut 4

Same fabric as piece 2

Add seam allowance to all pieces.

Alabama 5
Cut 4

Same fabric as piece 2

Alaska Pieced Border

The center star units are repeated in the four corners of the border design for the Alaska Pieced Border. Use this design on quilt centers with pieced stars and challenge yourself with the placement of colors.

Border Unit 1: 3" x 7 1/2"—24 per side
Border Unit 2: 3" x 7 1/2"—2 per side
Corner Unit: 7 1/2" x 7 1/2"—4 corners needed

Border is shown with the star pattern for Royal Star of Alaska. The pattern for the star is available in *Royal Stars of the States*, also published by House of White Birches. See ordering information on Page 159.

Alaska Pieced Border
Placement Diagram
Star Center 75" x 75"
Add 1 1/2" borders—78" x 78"
With Borders 93" x 93"

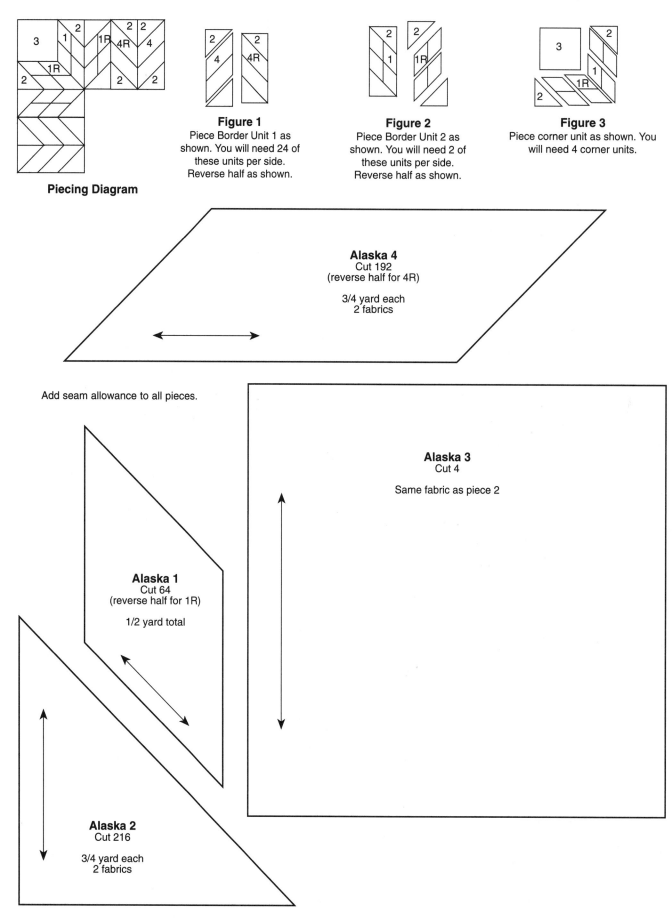

Piecing Diagram

Figure 1
Piece Border Unit 1 as shown. You will need 24 of these units per side. Reverse half as shown.

Figure 2
Piece Border Unit 2 as shown. You will need 2 of these units per side. Reverse half as shown.

Figure 3
Piece corner unit as shown. You will need 4 corner units.

Alaska 4
Cut 192
(reverse half for 4R)

3/4 yard each
2 fabrics

Add seam allowance to all pieces.

Alaska 3
Cut 4

Same fabric as piece 2

Alaska 1
Cut 64
(reverse half for 1R)

1/2 yard total

Alaska 2
Cut 216

3/4 yard each
2 fabrics

Arizona Pieced Border

The border design given is a 9 1/2" x 9 1/2" star block. Seven of these blocks finish at 66 1/2" long. The Royal Star of Arizona finishes at 66". If using this star design as a border for the Arizona center, make the corner squares and side fill-in triangles each 1/4" larger than directed. Trim your finished center to fit the pieced border.

Border Unit 1: 9 1/2" x 9 1/2"—7 per side
Corner Unit: 9 1/2" x 9 1/2"—4 corners needed

Border is shown with the star pattern for Royal Star of Arizona. The pattern for the star is available in *Royal Stars of the States*, also published by House of White Birches. See ordering information on Page 159.

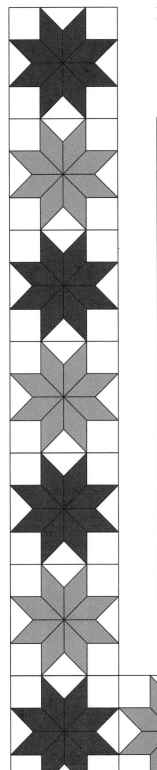

Arizona Pieced Border
Placement Diagram
Star Center 66" x 66"
With Borders 85 1/2" x 85 1/2"

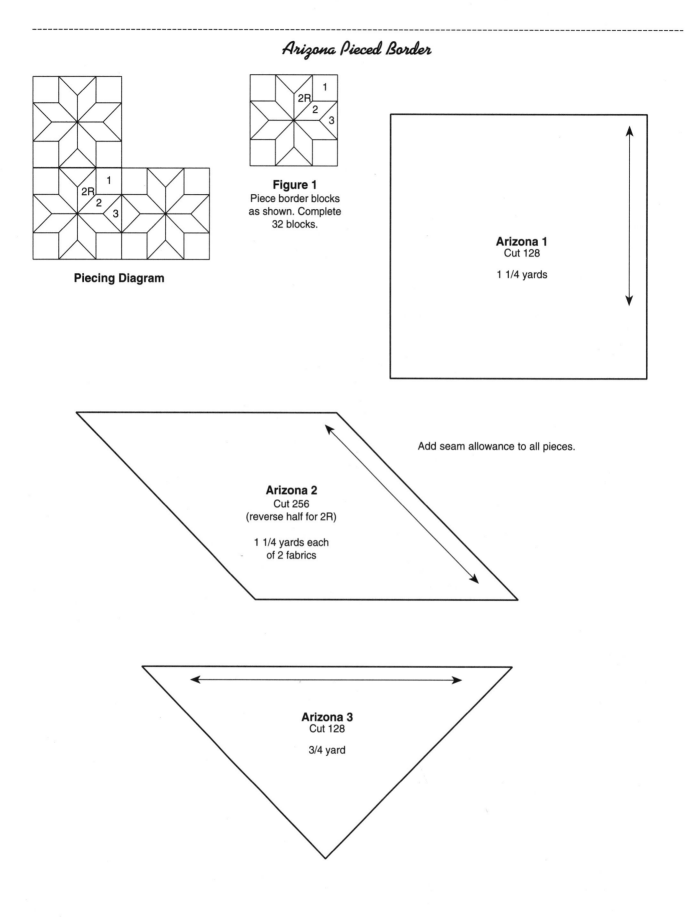

Piecing Diagram

Figure 1
Piece border blocks
as shown. Complete
32 blocks.

Arizona 1
Cut 128

1 1/4 yards

Add seam allowance to all pieces.

Arizona 2
Cut 256
(reverse half for 2R)

1 1/4 yards each
of 2 fabrics

Arizona 3
Cut 128

3/4 yard

Arkansas Pieced Border

The Arkansas border design was created to fit on an unusual size quilt. Refer to Figure 3 to use on an irregular-shaped center. This design may also be used on any square or rectangular quilt using pieced sections as is shown on the sides of the quilt in the colored drawing.

Border Unit 1: 4" x 9"—15 per short side and 17 per long side
Corner Unit: Irregular shape—4 corners needed

Border is shown with the star pattern for Royal Star of Arkansas. The pattern for the star is available in *Royal Stars of the States*, also published by House of White Birches. See ordering information on Page 159.

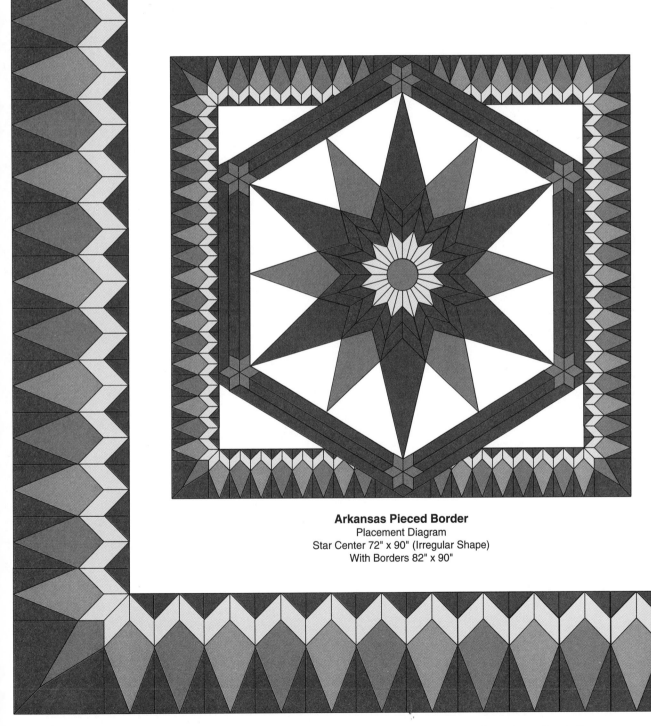

Arkansas Pieced Border
Placement Diagram
Star Center 72" x 90" (Irregular Shape)
With Borders 82" x 90"

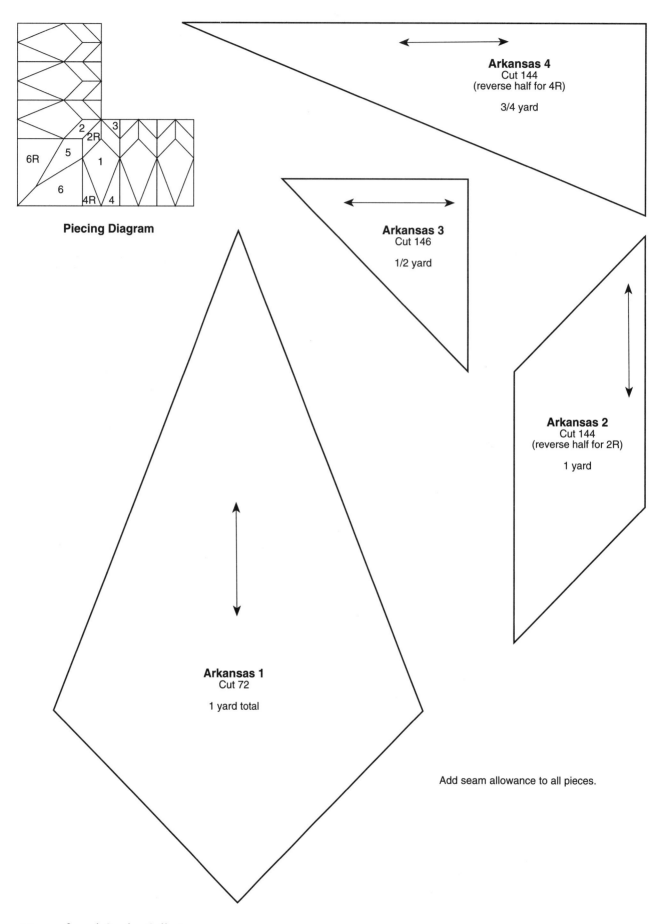

Piecing Diagram

Arkansas 4
Cut 144
(reverse half for 4R)

3/4 yard

Arkansas 3
Cut 146

1/2 yard

Arkansas 2
Cut 144
(reverse half for 2R)

1 yard

Arkansas 1
Cut 72

1 yard total

Add seam allowance to all pieces.

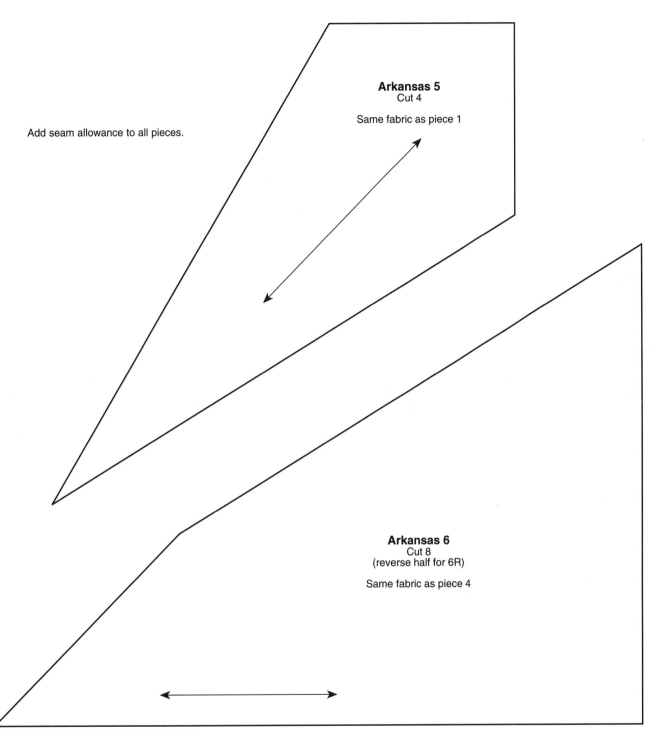

Add seam allowance to all pieces.

Arkansas 5
Cut 4

Same fabric as piece 1

Arkansas 6
Cut 8
(reverse half for 6R)

Same fabric as piece 4

California Pieced Border

Use this border design on any quilt center with sharp-angled pieces to make a striking finish to the edges. Repeat the colors from the center on the outside with the strongest colors in the narrow-angled pieces to balance the design.

Border Unit 1: 10" wide—8 per side
Border Unit 2: 10" wide—9 per side
Corner Unit: Irregular shape—4 corners needed

Border is shown with the star pattern for Royal Star of California. The pattern for the star is available in *Royal Stars of the States*, also published by House of White Birches. See ordering information on Page 159.

California Pieced Border
Placement Diagram
Star Center 72" x 72"
With Borders 92" x 92"

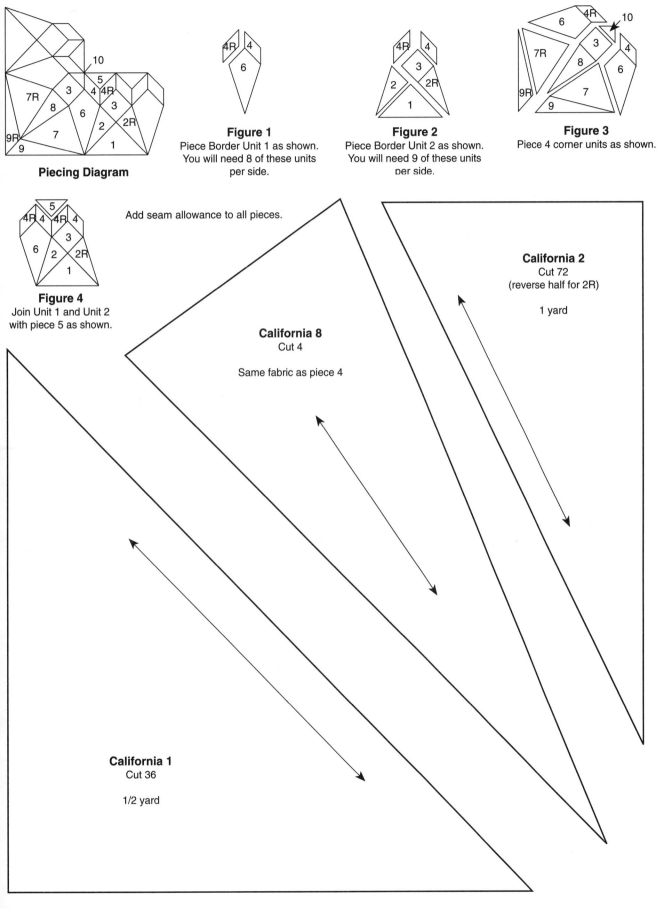

Piecing Diagram

Figure 1
Piece Border Unit 1 as shown.
You will need 8 of these units
per side.

Figure 2
Piece Border Unit 2 as shown.
You will need 9 of these units
per side.

Figure 3
Piece 4 corner units as shown.

Figure 4
Join Unit 1 and Unit 2
with piece 5 as shown.

Add seam allowance to all pieces.

California 8
Cut 4

Same fabric as piece 4

California 2
Cut 72
(reverse half for 2R)

1 yard

California 1
Cut 36

1/2 yard

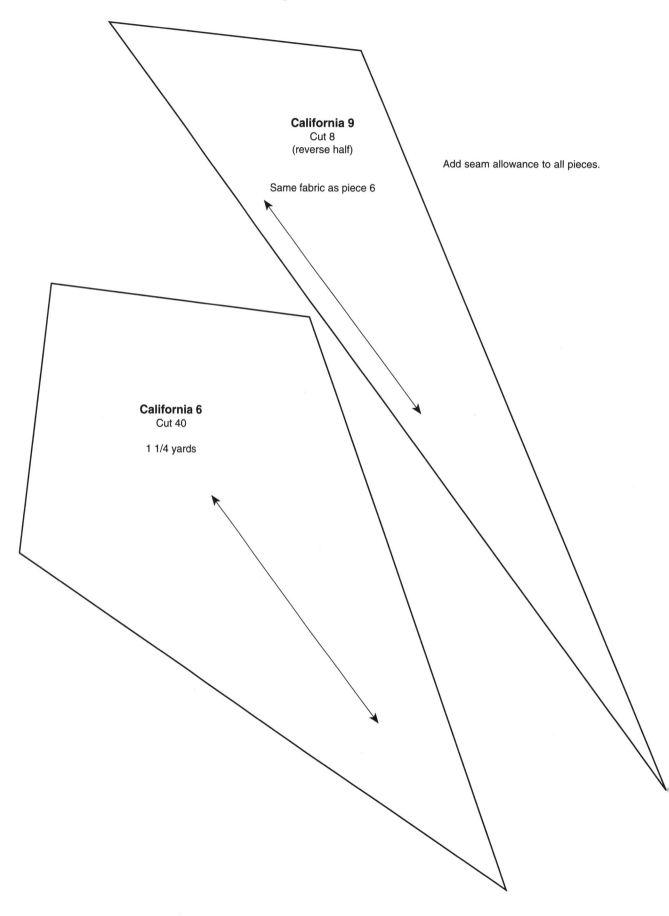

California 9
Cut 8
(reverse half)

Same fabric as piece 6

Add seam allowance to all pieces.

California 6
Cut 40

1 1/4 yards

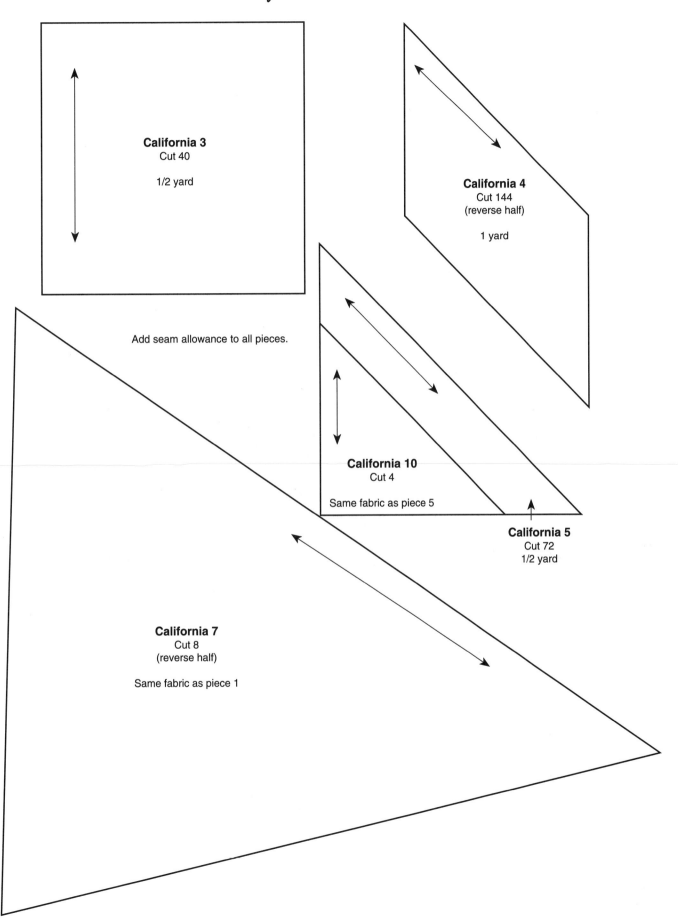

California 3
Cut 40

1/2 yard

California 4
Cut 144
(reverse half)

1 yard

Add seam allowance to all pieces.

California 10
Cut 4

Same fabric as piece 5

California 5
Cut 72
1/2 yard

California 7
Cut 8
(reverse half)

Same fabric as piece 1

Colorado Pieced Border

If you like complicated patterns, try this design on a quilt center made with arrow-shaped pieces. The small angles with fine points are a challenge for even the most experienced piecer.

Border Unit 1: 6" x 10"—13 per side
Border Unit 2: 6" x 10"—12 per side
Corner Unit: Irregular shape—4 corners needed

Border is shown with the star pattern for Royal Star of Colorado. The pattern for the star is available in *Royal Stars of the States*, also published by House of White Birches. See ordering information on Page 159.

Colorado Pieced Border
Placement Diagram
Star Center 72" x 72"
With Borders 92" x 92"

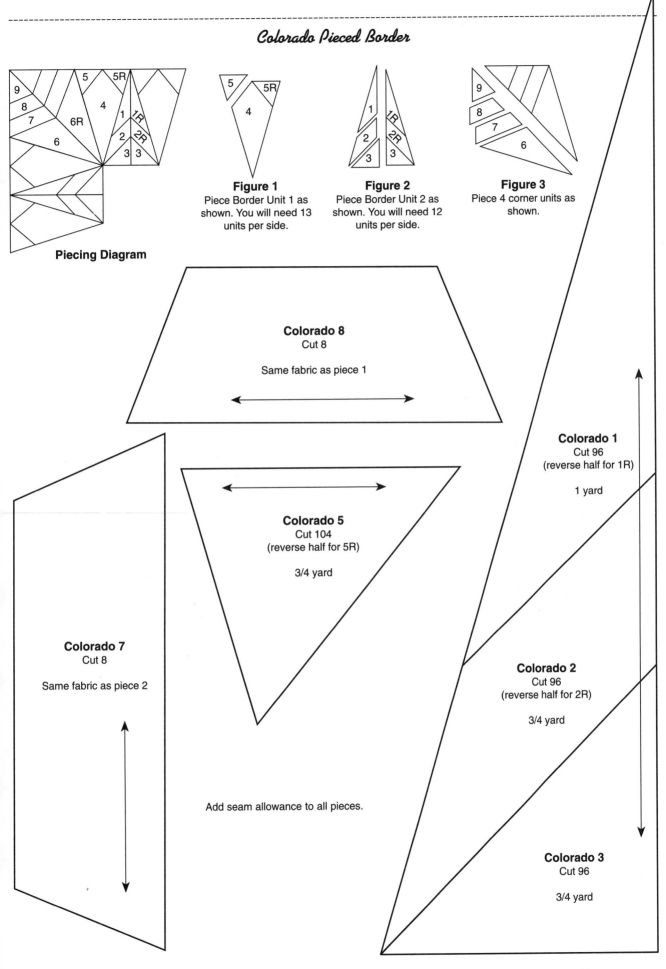

Piecing Diagram

Figure 1
Piece Border Unit 1 as shown. You will need 13 units per side.

Figure 2
Piece Border Unit 2 as shown. You will need 12 units per side.

Figure 3
Piece 4 corner units as shown.

Colorado 8
Cut 8

Same fabric as piece 1

Colorado 5
Cut 104
(reverse half for 5R)

3/4 yard

Colorado 7
Cut 8

Same fabric as piece 2

Add seam allowance to all pieces.

Colorado 1
Cut 96
(reverse half for 1R)

1 yard

Colorado 2
Cut 96
(reverse half for 2R)

3/4 yard

Colorado 3
Cut 96

3/4 yard

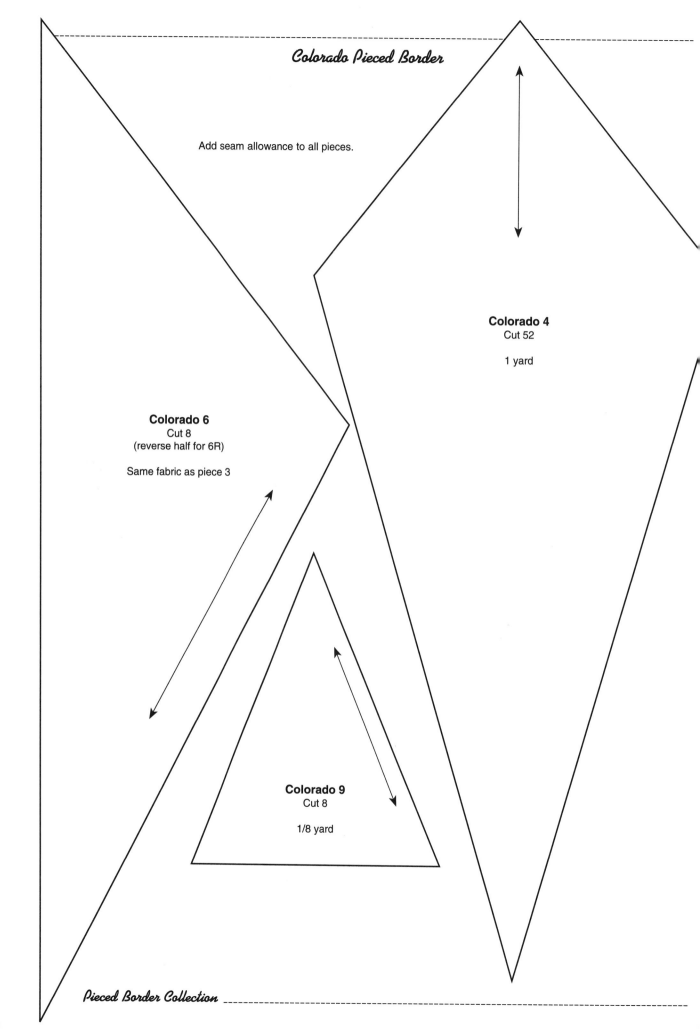

Add seam allowance to all pieces.

Colorado 4
Cut 52

1 yard

Colorado 6
Cut 8
(reverse half for 6R)

Same fabric as piece 3

Colorado 9
Cut 8

1/8 yard

Connecticut Pieced Border

If you are looking for a challenge, try piecing this border design. Beginners or the faint of heart should not attempt this pattern! Hand-piecing is recommended.

Border Unit: Irregular shape; 8" wide—19 per side
Corner Unit: Irregular shape—4 corners needed

Border is shown with the star pattern for Royal Star of Connecticut. The pattern for the star is available in *Royal Stars of the States*, also published by House of White Birches. See ordering information on Page 159.

Connecticut Pieced Border
Placement Diagram
Star Center 72" x 72"
Add 2" borders—76" x 76"
With Borders 92" x 92"

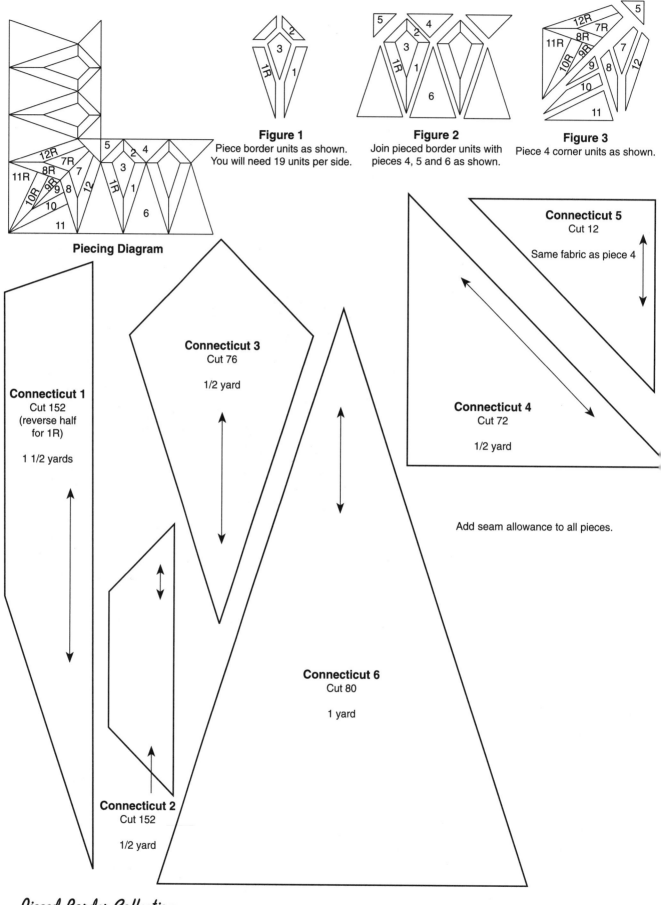

Figure 1
Piece border units as shown.
You will need 19 units per side.

Figure 2
Join pieced border units with
pieces 4, 5 and 6 as shown.

Figure 3
Piece 4 corner units as shown.

Piecing Diagram

Connecticut 5
Cut 12

Same fabric as piece 4

Connecticut 4
Cut 72

1/2 yard

Connecticut 3
Cut 76

1/2 yard

Connecticut 1
Cut 152
(reverse half
for 1R)

1 1/2 yards

Add seam allowance to all pieces.

Connecticut 6
Cut 80

1 yard

Connecticut 2
Cut 152

1/2 yard

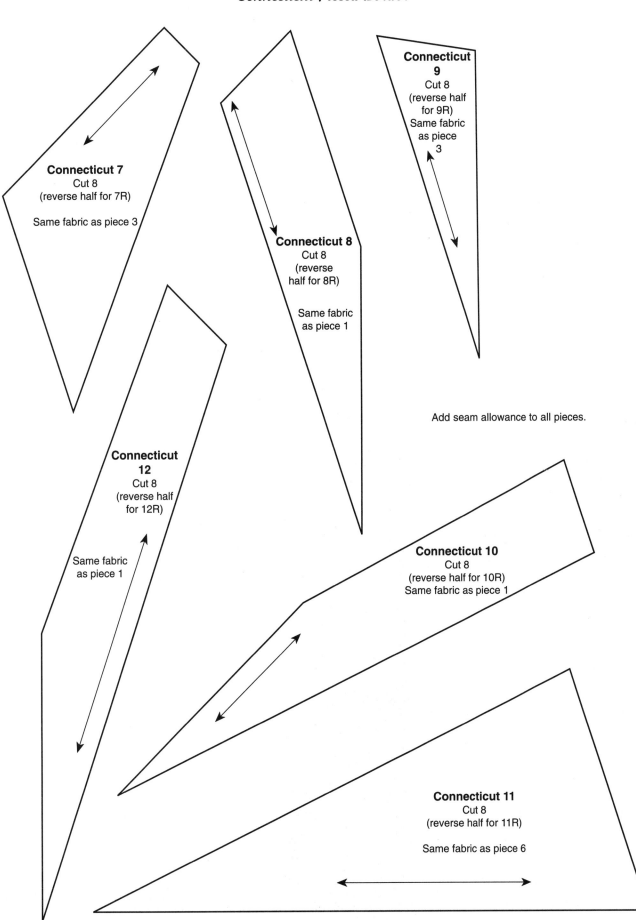

Connecticut 7
Cut 8
(reverse half for 7R)

Same fabric as piece 3

Connecticut 8
Cut 8
(reverse
half for 8R)

Same fabric
as piece 1

Connecticut 9
Cut 8
(reverse half
for 9R)
Same fabric
as piece 3

Add seam allowance to all pieces.

Connecticut 12
Cut 8
(reverse half
for 12R)

Same fabric
as piece 1

Connecticut 10
Cut 8
(reverse half for 10R)
Same fabric as piece 1

Connecticut 11
Cut 8
(reverse half for 11R)

Same fabric as piece 6

Delaware Pieced Border

This border was designed for the Royal Star of Delaware, which has a 75" center. This design fits a 76" center. A 1/2" (finished size) border strip should be added all around a 75" center before adding this border.

Border Unit: 8" wide—9 per side
Corner Unit: Irregular shape—4 corners needed

Border is shown with the star pattern for Royal Star of Delaware. The pattern for the star is available in *Royal Stars of the States*, also published by House of White Birches. See ordering information on Page 159.

Delaware Pieced Border
Placement Diagram
Star Center 75" x 75"
Add 1/2" borders—76" x 76"
With Borders 92" x 92"

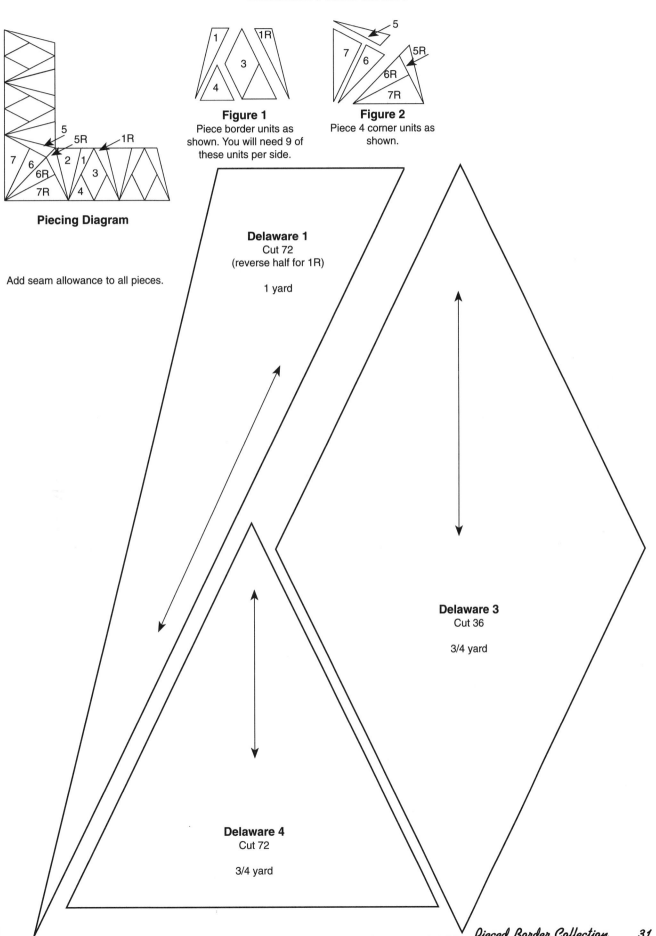

Piecing Diagram

Add seam allowance to all pieces.

Figure 1
Piece border units as shown. You will need 9 of these units per side.

Figure 2
Piece 4 corner units as shown.

Delaware 1
Cut 72
(reverse half for 1R)

1 yard

Delaware 3
Cut 36

3/4 yard

Delaware 4
Cut 72

3/4 yard

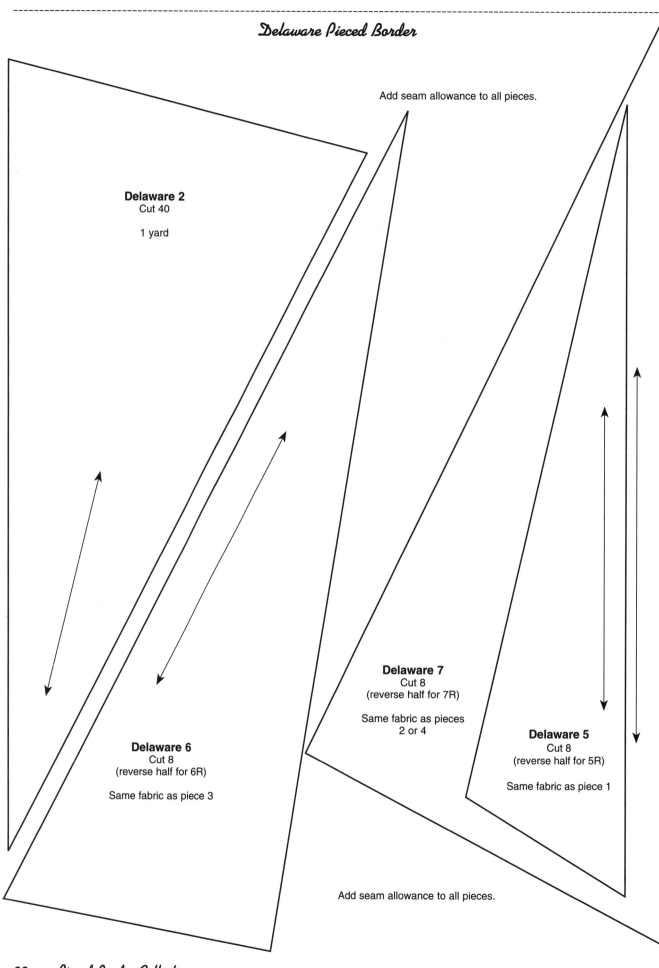

Add seam allowance to all pieces.

Delaware 2
Cut 40

1 yard

Delaware 7
Cut 8
(reverse half for 7R)

Same fabric as pieces
2 or 4

Delaware 5
Cut 8
(reverse half for 5R)

Same fabric as piece 1

Delaware 6
Cut 8
(reverse half for 6R)

Same fabric as piece 3

Add seam allowance to all pieces.

Florida Pieced Border

This border design has darker colors pointing toward the center and lighter colors on the outside edge. Binding the edges of your quilt with the darkest color will contain the design and accent the edge.

Border Unit 1: 8" base x 8" wide—10 per side
Border Unit 2: 8" base x 8" wide—9 per side

Border is shown with the star pattern for Royal Star of Florida. The pattern for the star is available in *Royal Stars of the States*, also published by House of White Birches. See ordering information on Page 159.

Florida Pieced Border
Placement Diagram
Star Center 72" x 72"
With Borders 88" x 88"

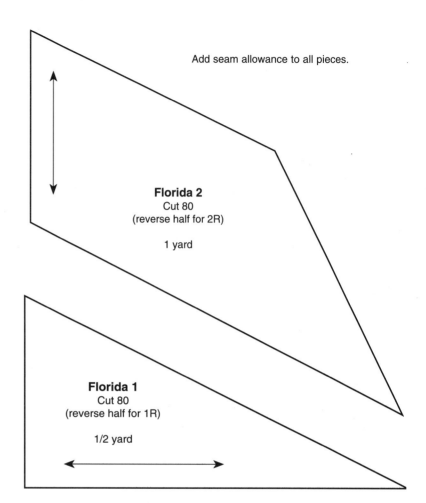

Add seam allowance to all pieces.

Florida 2
Cut 80
(reverse half for 2R)

1 yard

Florida 1
Cut 80
(reverse half for 1R)

1/2 yard

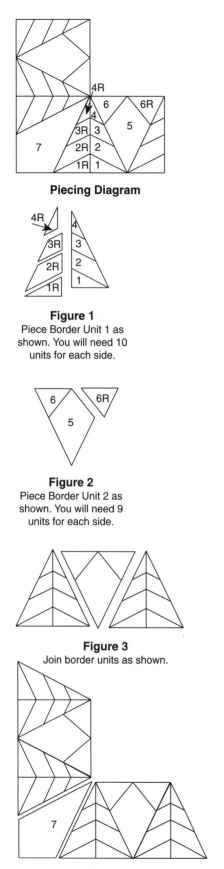

Piecing Diagram

Figure 1
Piece Border Unit 1 as shown. You will need 10 units for each side.

Figure 2
Piece Border Unit 2 as shown. You will need 9 units for each side.

Figure 3
Join border units as shown.

Figure 4
Join border units at corners with piece 7.

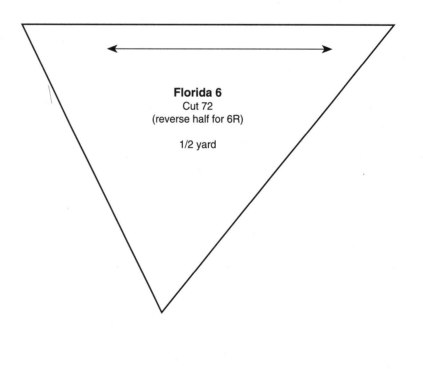

Florida 6
Cut 72
(reverse half for 6R)

1/2 yard

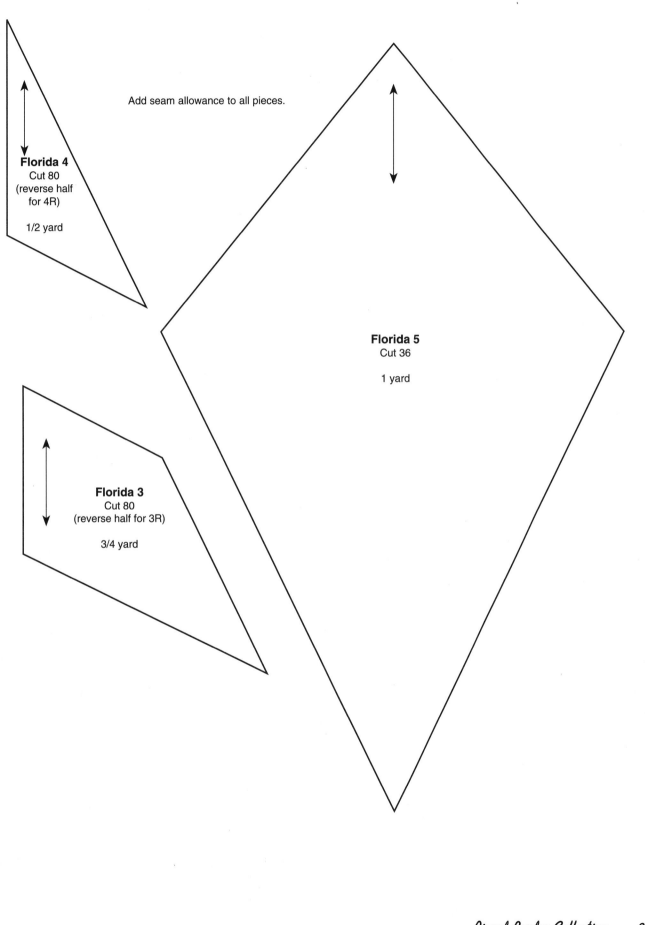

Add seam allowance to all pieces.

Florida 4
Cut 80
(reverse half
for 4R)

1/2 yard

Florida 5
Cut 36

1 yard

Florida 3
Cut 80
(reverse half for 3R)

3/4 yard

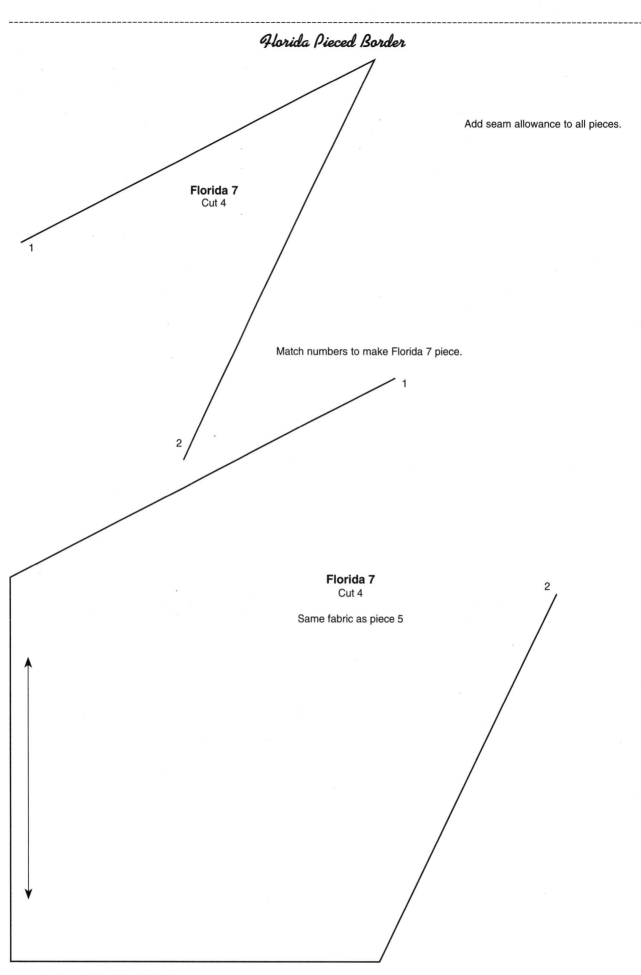

Add seam allowance to all pieces.

Florida 7
Cut 4

1

Match numbers to make Florida 7 piece.

1

2

Florida 7
Cut 4

Same fabric as piece 5

2

Georgia Pieced Border

Unlike many of the other border designs in this book, this one is not pieced in units which are joined to create the design. There are star units just like those used in the center of the quilt repeated on the outside edges. The border could be turned with the star points facing toward the outside for a different look.

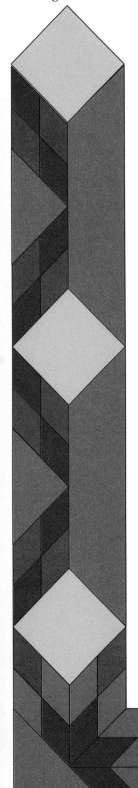

Border Unit: 6" star
Border: 8 1/2" wide

Border is shown with the star pattern for Royal Star of Georgia. The pattern for the star is available in *Royal Stars of the States*, also published by House of White Birches. See ordering information on Page 159.

Georgia Pieced Border
Placement Diagram
Star Center 67 1/2" x 67 1/2"
Add 3" borders—73 1/2" x 73 1/2"
With Borders 90 1/2" x 90 1/2"

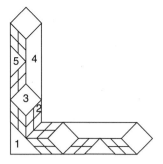

Piecing Diagram

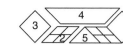

Figure 1
Piece border star unit as shown. You will need 6 of these units for each side and 4 for each corner.

Figure 2
Piece border units together as shown for each side. Add corner triangles after adding border strips to quilt center.

Add seam allowance to all pieces.

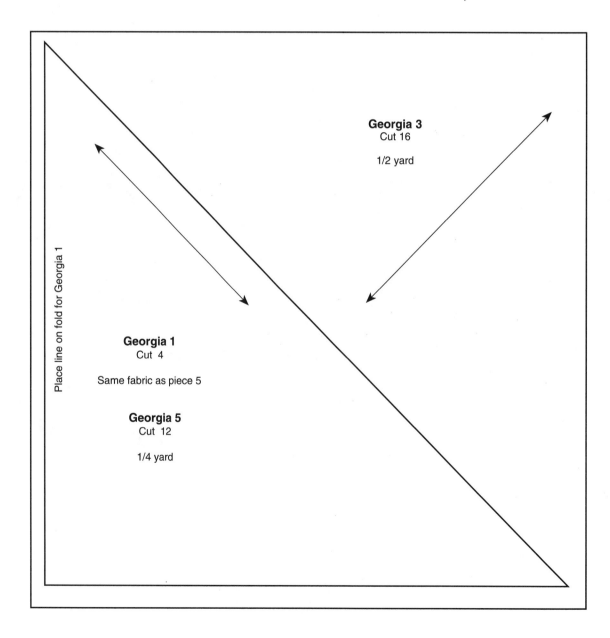

Place line on fold for Georgia 1

Georgia 3
Cut 16

1/2 yard

Georgia 1
Cut 4

Same fabric as piece 5

Georgia 5
Cut 12

1/4 yard

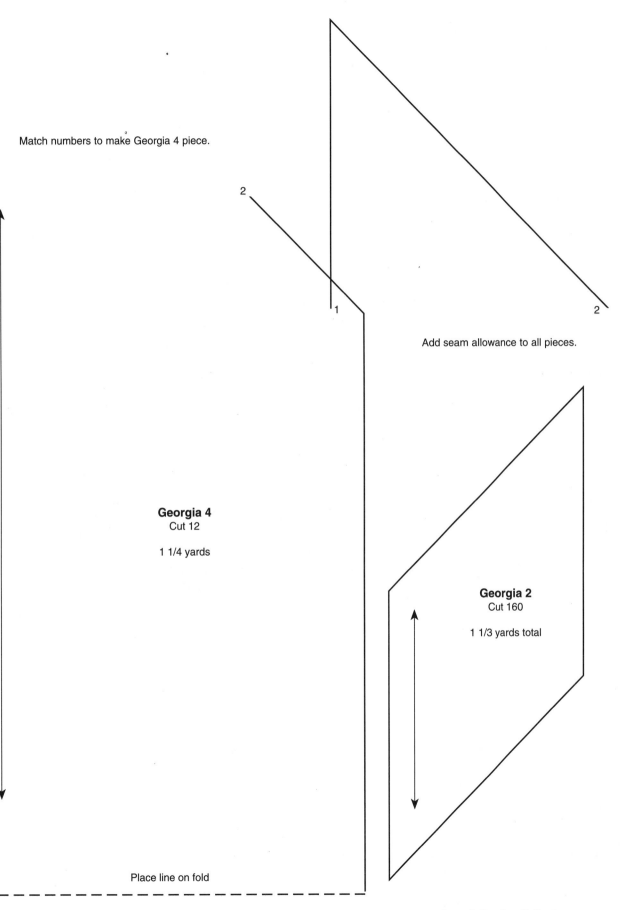

Match numbers to make Georgia 4 piece.

Add seam allowance to all pieces.

Georgia 4
Cut 12

1 1/4 yards

Georgia 2
Cut 160

1 1/3 yards total

Place line on fold

Hawaii Pieced Border

Placement of colors when using this border pattern could alter the dominant shapes. The wing-shaped pieces seem to pop out as it is shown, but if piece 3 were made in a darker color, it would create a definite shape which would stand out.

Border Unit: 4" x 8"—18 per side
Corner Unit: 8" x 8"—4 corners needed

Border is shown with the star pattern for Royal Star of Hawaii. The pattern for the star is available in *Royal Stars of the States*, also published by House of White Birches. See ordering information on Page 159.

Hawaii Pieced Border
Placement Diagram
Star Center 72" x 72"
With Borders 88" x 88"

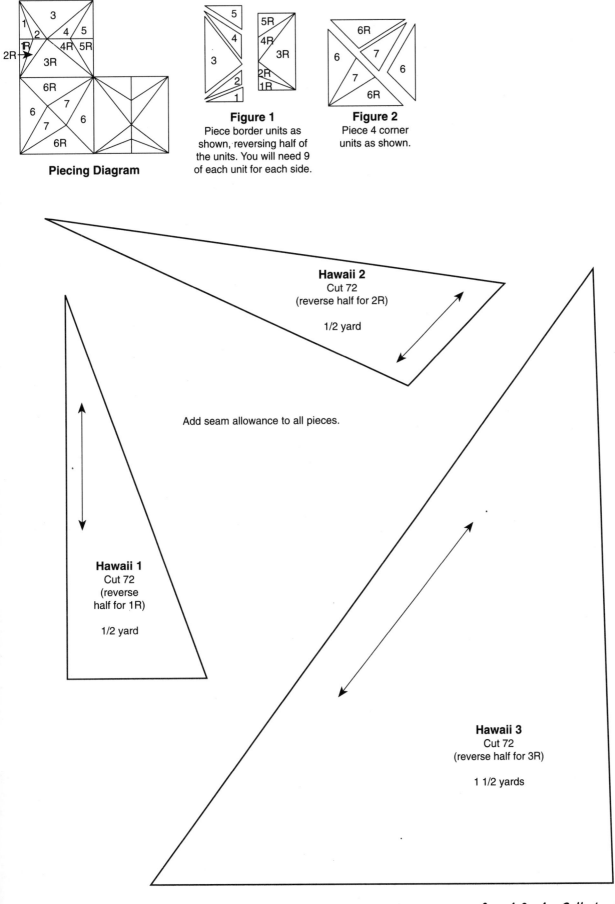

Piecing Diagram

Figure 1
Piece border units as
shown, reversing half of
the units. You will need 9
of each unit for each side.

Figure 2
Piece 4 corner
units as shown.

Hawaii 2
Cut 72
(reverse half for 2R)

1/2 yard

Add seam allowance to all pieces.

Hawaii 1
Cut 72
(reverse
half for 1R)

1/2 yard

Hawaii 3
Cut 72
(reverse half for 3R)

1 1/2 yards

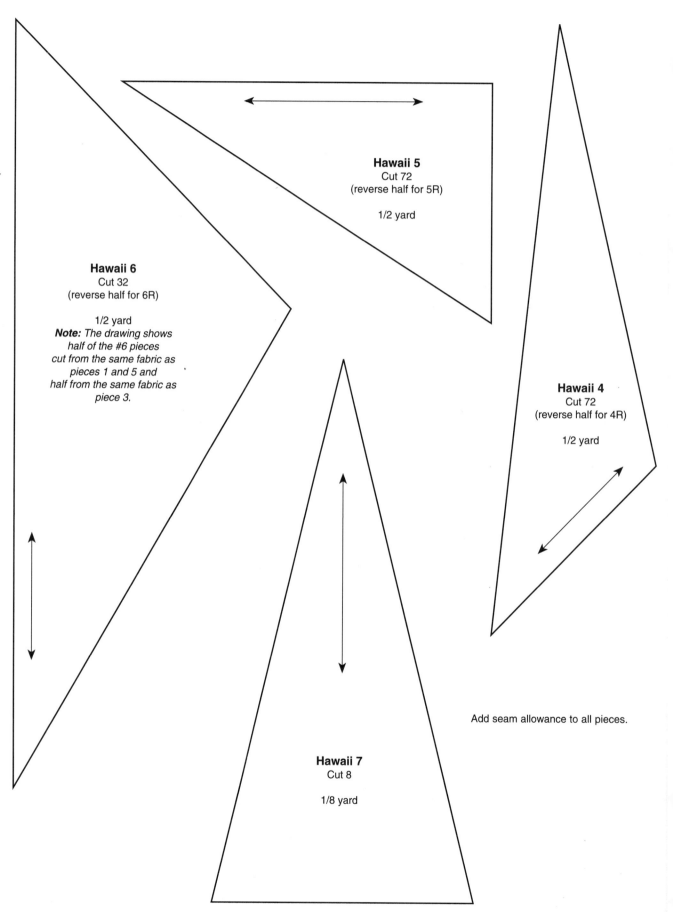

Hawaii 5
Cut 72
(reverse half for 5R)

1/2 yard

Hawaii 6
Cut 32
(reverse half for 6R)

1/2 yard
Note: *The drawing shows half of the #6 pieces cut from the same fabric as pieces 1 and 5 and half from the same fabric as piece 3.*

Hawaii 4
Cut 72
(reverse half for 4R)

1/2 yard

Add seam allowance to all pieces.

Hawaii 7
Cut 8

1/8 yard

Idaho Pieced Border

What a colorful border this design makes! The diamond is used to make large triangles which look like star points. This well-designed border could be used successfully on many quilts.

Border Unit 1: 4" x 8"—6 per side
Border Unit 2: 8" x 8"—5 per side
Border Unit 3: Irregular shape—2 per side
Corner Unit: Irregular shape—4 corners needed

Border is shown with the star pattern for Royal Star of Idaho. The pattern for the star is available in *Royal Stars of the States*, also published by House of White Birches. See ordering information on Page 159.

Idaho Pieced Border
Placement Diagram
Star Center 72" x 72"
With Borders 88" x 88"

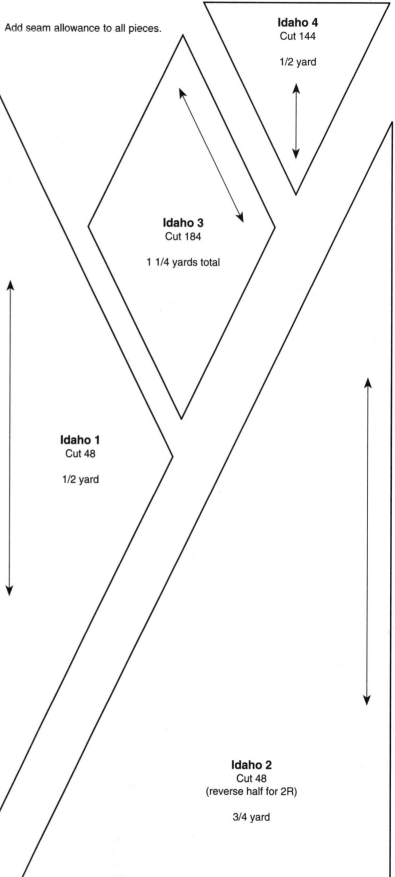

Add seam allowance to all pieces.

Idaho 4
Cut 144

1/2 yard

Idaho 3
Cut 184

1 1/4 yards total

Idaho 1
Cut 48

1/2 yard

Idaho 2
Cut 48
(reverse half for 2R)

3/4 yard

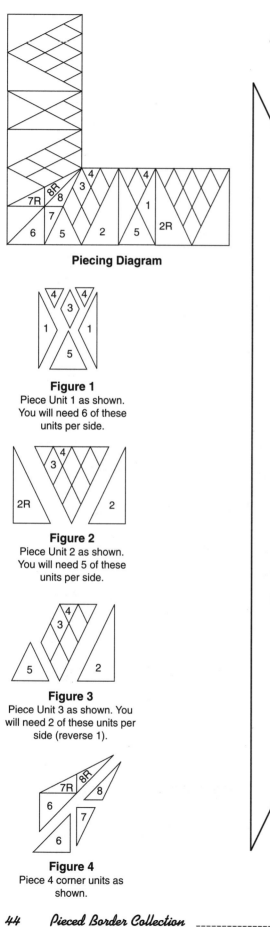

Piecing Diagram

Figure 1
Piece Unit 1 as shown.
You will need 6 of these
units per side.

Figure 2
Piece Unit 2 as shown.
You will need 5 of these
units per side.

Figure 3
Piece Unit 3 as shown. You
will need 2 of these units per
side (reverse 1).

Figure 4
Piece 4 corner units as
shown.

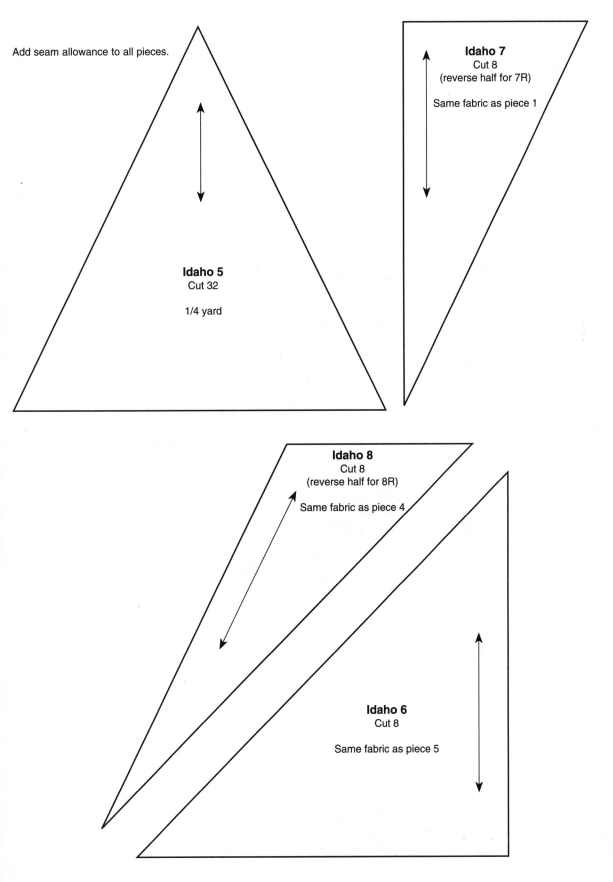

Add seam allowance to all pieces.

Idaho 5
Cut 32

1/4 yard

Idaho 7
Cut 8
(reverse half for 7R)

Same fabric as piece 1

Idaho 8
Cut 8
(reverse half for 8R)

Same fabric as piece 4

Idaho 6
Cut 8

Same fabric as piece 5

Illinois Pieced Border

In the border designed for the Illinois Star, the wing-shaped piece 2 is repeated in the points of the border units. The corner shapes are not squares, but use part of the border unit. These corners are the perfect finish for this border design.

Border Unit 1: 7 1/2" x 8"—8 per side
Border Unit 2: 8"-wide irregular shape—2 per side
Corner Unit: Irregular shape—4 corners needed

Border is shown with the star pattern for Royal Star of Illinois. The pattern for the star is available in *Royal Stars of the States*, also published by House of White Birches. See ordering information on Page 159.

Illinois Pieced Border
Placement Diagram
Star Center 75" x 75"
With Borders 91" x 91"

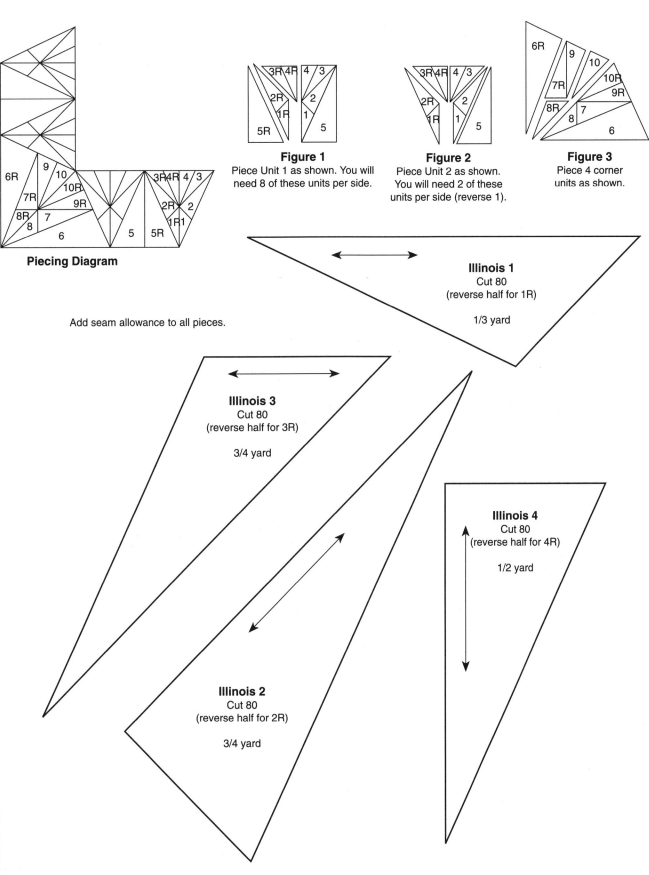

Figure 1
Piece Unit 1 as shown. You will
need 8 of these units per side.

Figure 2
Piece Unit 2 as shown.
You will need 2 of these
units per side (reverse 1).

Figure 3
Piece 4 corner
units as shown.

Piecing Diagram

Add seam allowance to all pieces.

Illinois 1
Cut 80
(reverse half for 1R)

1/3 yard

Illinois 3
Cut 80
(reverse half for 3R)

3/4 yard

Illinois 4
Cut 80
(reverse half for 4R)

1/2 yard

Illinois 2
Cut 80
(reverse half for 2R)

3/4 yard

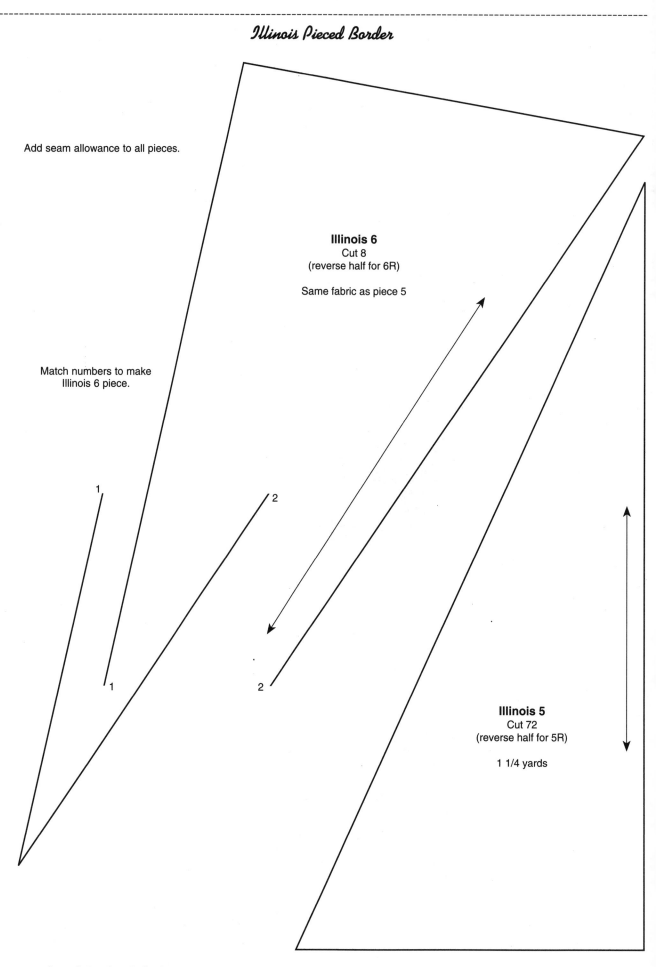

Add seam allowance to all pieces.

Illinois 6
Cut 8
(reverse half for 6R)

Same fabric as piece 5

Match numbers to make
Illinois 6 piece.

1

2

1

2

Illinois 5
Cut 72
(reverse half for 5R)

1 1/4 yards

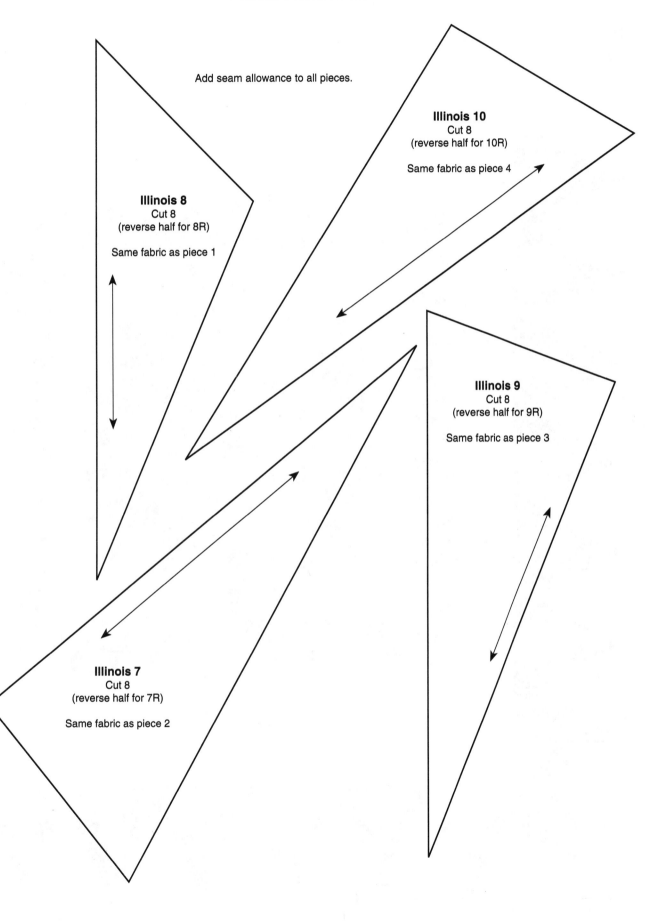

Add seam allowance to all pieces.

Illinois 10
Cut 8
(reverse half for 10R)

Same fabric as piece 4

Illinois 8
Cut 8
(reverse half for 8R)

Same fabric as piece 1

Illinois 9
Cut 8
(reverse half for 9R)

Same fabric as piece 3

Illinois 7
Cut 8
(reverse half for 7R)

Same fabric as piece 2

Indiana Pieced Border

The very sharp angles on this border design make it a bit tricky to piece. Be very careful when cutting and stitching—accuracy will produce perfect results.

Border Unit: 8" x 10"—7 per side
Corner Unit: Irregular shape—4 corners

Border is shown with the star pattern for Royal Star of Indiana. The pattern for the star is available in *Royal Stars of the States*, also published by House of White Birches. See ordering information on Page 159.

Indiana Pieced Border
Placement Diagram
Star Center 72" x 72"
With Borders 92" x 92"

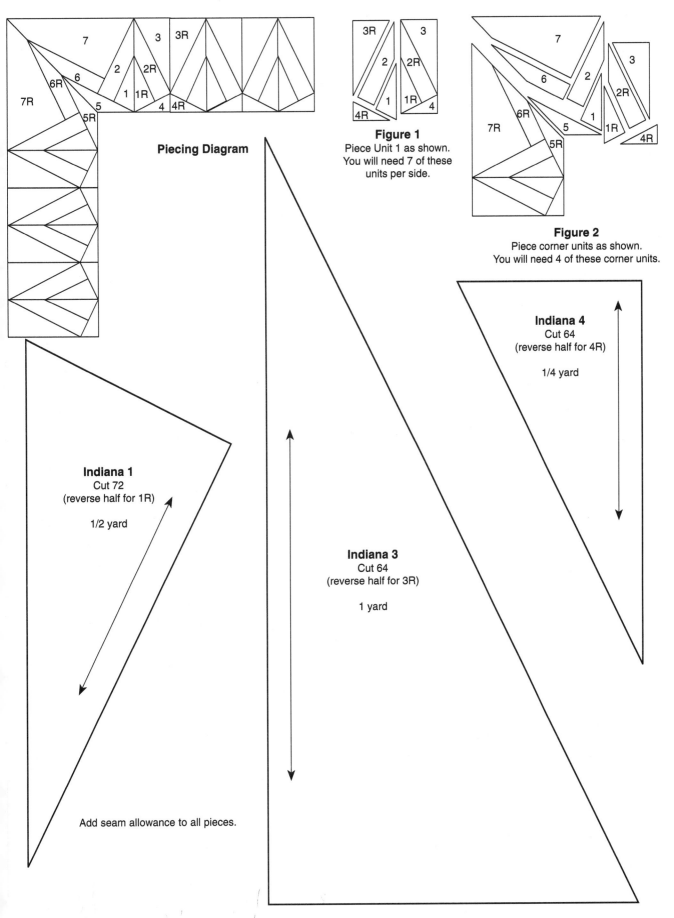

Piecing Diagram

Figure 1
Piece Unit 1 as shown.
You will need 7 of these
units per side.

Figure 2
Piece corner units as shown.
You will need 4 of these corner units.

Indiana 1
Cut 72
(reverse half for 1R)

1/2 yard

Indiana 4
Cut 64
(reverse half for 4R)

1/4 yard

Indiana 3
Cut 64
(reverse half for 3R)

1 yard

Add seam allowance to all pieces.

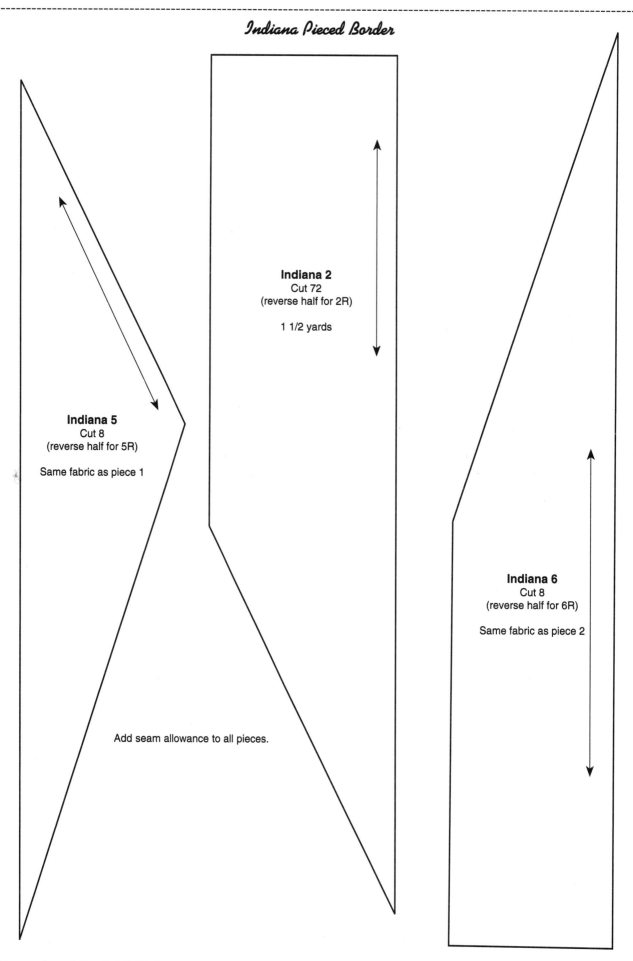

Indiana 2
Cut 72
(reverse half for 2R)

1 1/2 yards

Indiana 5
Cut 8
(reverse half for 5R)

Same fabric as piece 1

Indiana 6
Cut 8
(reverse half for 6R)

Same fabric as piece 2

Add seam allowance to all pieces.

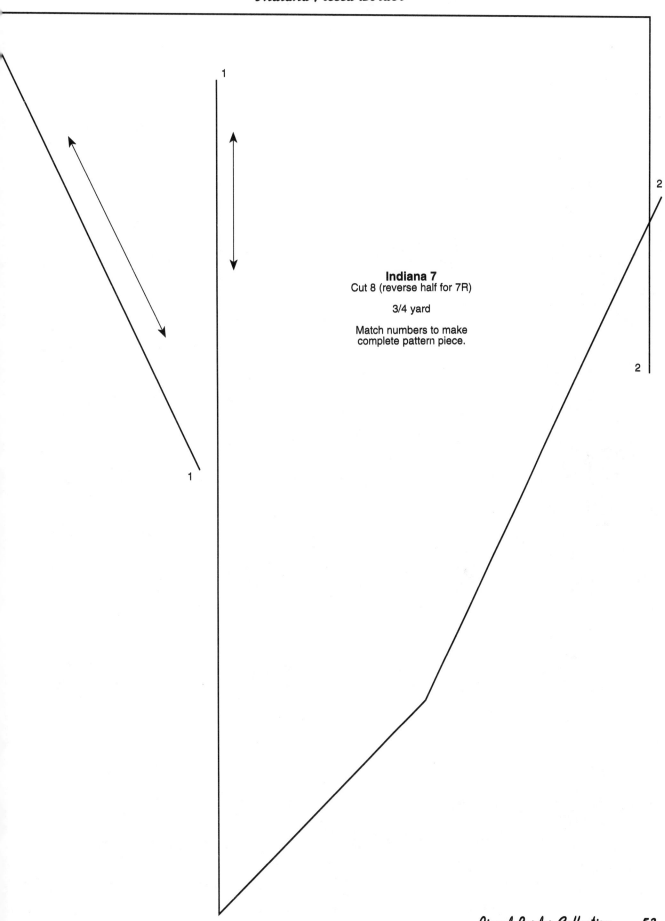

Indiana 7
Cut 8 (reverse half for 7R)

3/4 yard

Match numbers to make
complete pattern piece.

Iowa Pieced Border

The pieces used in this border design give a zigzag appearance as they move around the quilt. The three pieced units that make up the design use angled pieces to create the illusion of movement.

Border Unit 1: 8" x 8"—8 per side
Border Unit 2: 4" x 8"—2 per side
Corner Unit: 8" x 8"—4 corners

Border is shown with the star pattern for Royal Star of Iowa. The pattern for the star is available in *Royal Stars of the States*, also published by House of White Birches. See ordering information on Page 159.

Iowa Pieced Border
Placement Diagram
Star Center 72" x 72"
With Borders 88" x 88"

Iowa Pieced Border

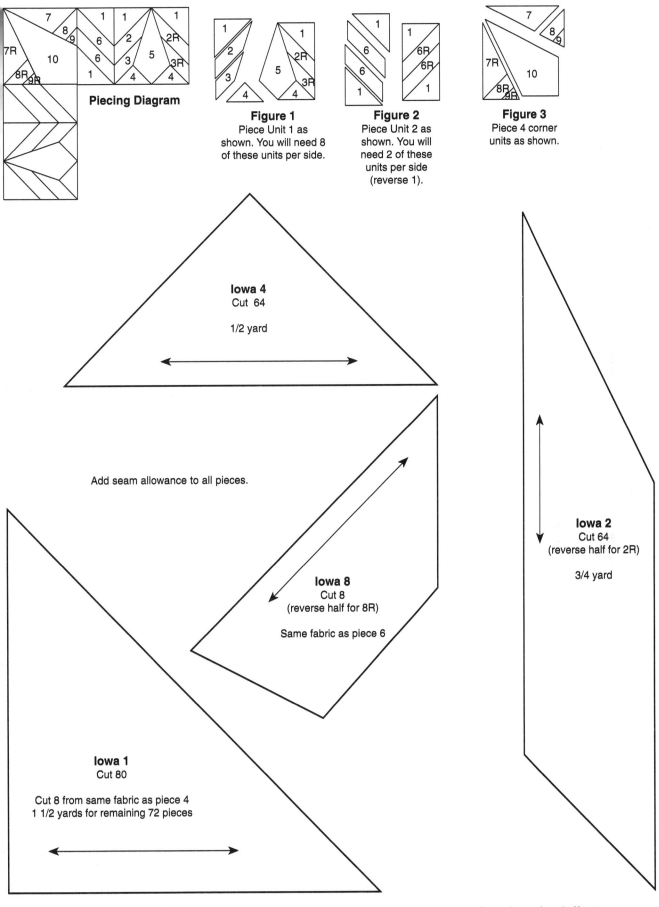

Piecing Diagram

Figure 1
Piece Unit 1 as
shown. You will need 8
of these units per side.

Figure 2
Piece Unit 2 as
shown. You will
need 2 of these
units per side
(reverse 1).

Figure 3
Piece 4 corner
units as shown.

Iowa 4
Cut 64

1/2 yard

Add seam allowance to all pieces.

Iowa 8
Cut 8
(reverse half for 8R)

Same fabric as piece 6

Iowa 2
Cut 64
(reverse half for 2R)

3/4 yard

Iowa 1
Cut 80

Cut 8 from same fabric as piece 4
1 1/2 yards for remaining 72 pieces

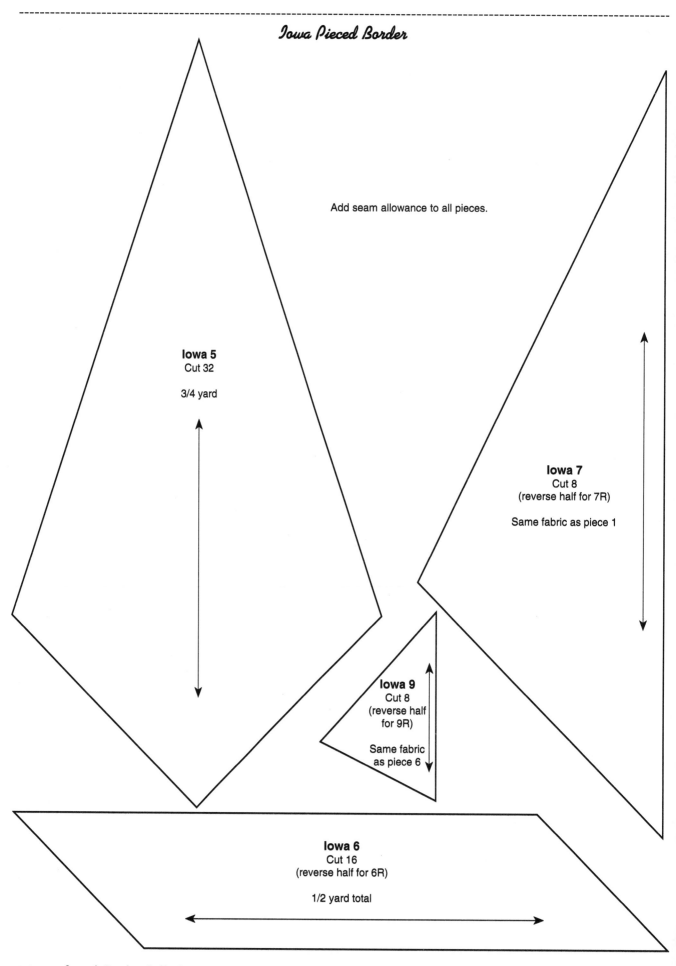

Add seam allowance to all pieces.

Iowa 5
Cut 32

3/4 yard

Iowa 7
Cut 8
(reverse half for 7R)

Same fabric as piece 1

Iowa 9
Cut 8
(reverse half
for 9R)

Same fabric
as piece 6

Iowa 6
Cut 16
(reverse half for 6R)

1/2 yard total

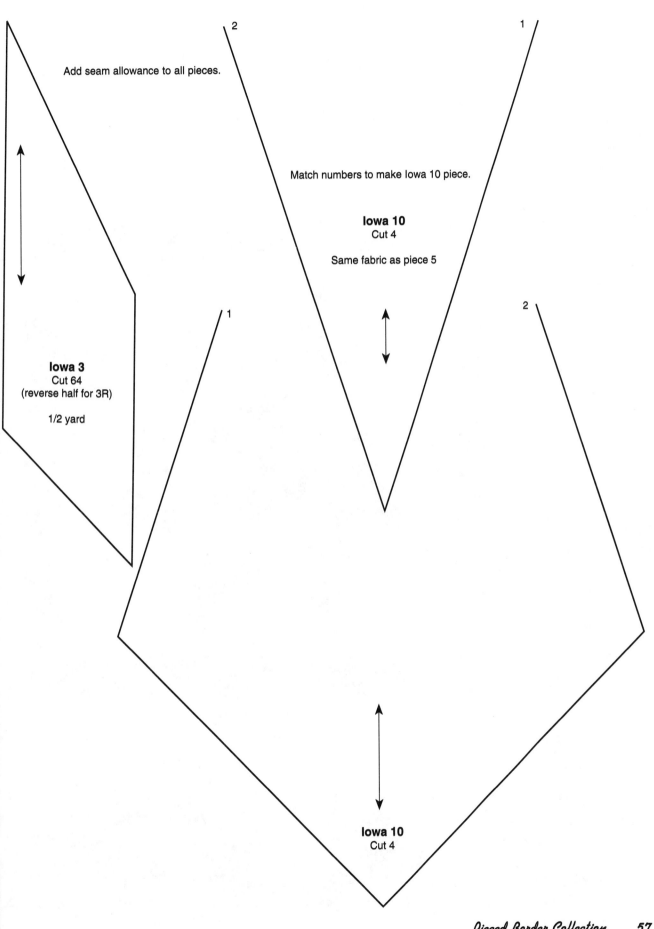

Add seam allowance to all pieces.

Match numbers to make Iowa 10 piece.

Iowa 10
Cut 4

Same fabric as piece 5

Iowa 3
Cut 64
(reverse half for 3R)

1/2 yard

Iowa 10
Cut 4

Kansas Pieced Border

Repeating the darkest color in your quilt in the diamond-shaped border units makes this a striking border design. To make the 8" x 11" design work with a 66" center, a 5 1/4" border strip was added all around. Adjust to use this border on a quilt of a different size.

Border Unit: 8" x 11"—6 per side
Corner Unit: Irregular shape; 8" wide—4 corners

Border is shown with the star pattern for Royal Star of Kansas. The pattern for the star is available in *Royal Stars of the States*, also published by House of White Birches. See ordering information on Page 159.

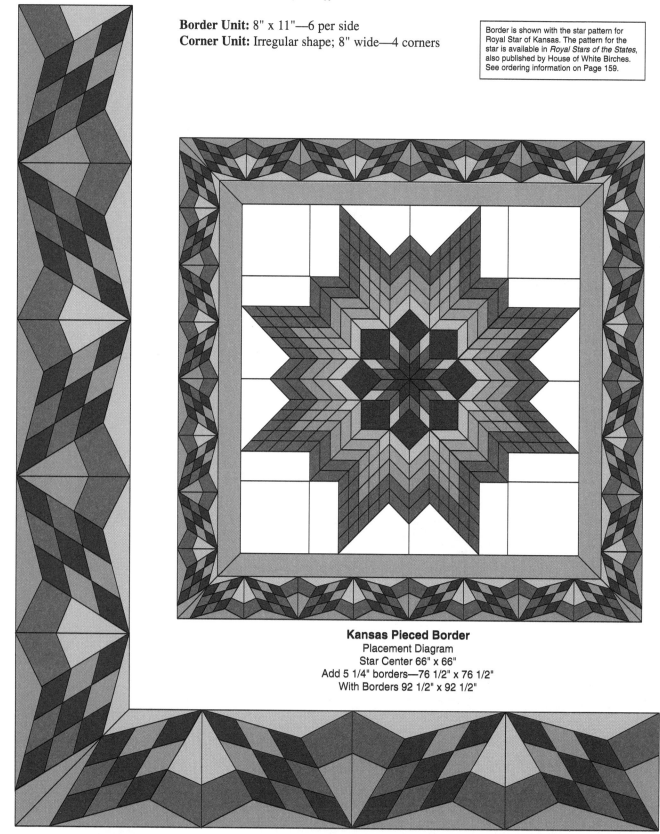

Kansas Pieced Border
Placement Diagram
Star Center 66" x 66"
Add 5 1/4" borders—76 1/2" x 76 1/2"
With Borders 92 1/2" x 92 1/2"

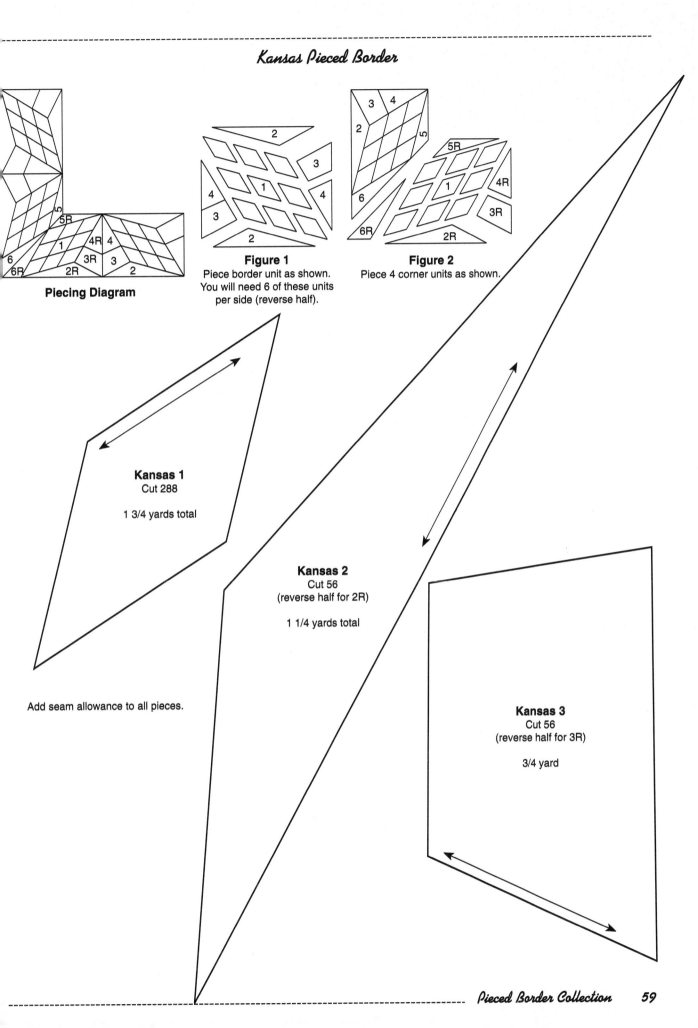

Piecing Diagram

Figure 1
Piece border unit as shown.
You will need 6 of these units
per side (reverse half).

Figure 2
Piece 4 corner units as shown.

Kansas 1
Cut 288

1 3/4 yards total

Add seam allowance to all pieces.

Kansas 2
Cut 56
(reverse half for 2R)

1 1/4 yards total

Kansas 3
Cut 56
(reverse half for 3R)

3/4 yard

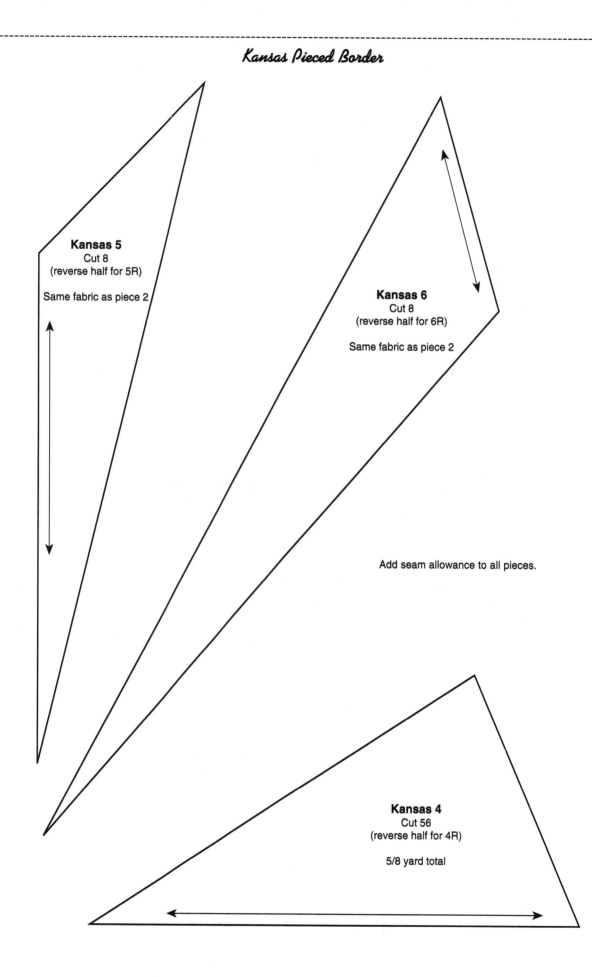

Kansas 5
Cut 8
(reverse half for 5R)

Same fabric as piece 2

Kansas 6
Cut 8
(reverse half for 6R)

Same fabric as piece 2

Add seam allowance to all pieces.

Kansas 4
Cut 56
(reverse half for 4R)

5/8 yard total

Kentucky Pieced Border

Sew squares to make triangles and set them together in a stair-like shape to make this simple pieced border. Because it uses a 12" unit, it is easy to fit it to many sized quilts, especially when using 12" blocks in the quilt center. As shown on the Kentucky star, the triangle/square units are repeated from the center. Because many pieced blocks are made with these units, this border is one of the most versatile.

Border Unit: 8" x 12"—5 per side
Corner Unit: Irregular shape—4 corners

Border is shown with the star pattern for Royal Star of Kentucky. The pattern for the star is available in *Royal Stars of the States*, also published by House of White Birches. See ordering information on Page 159.

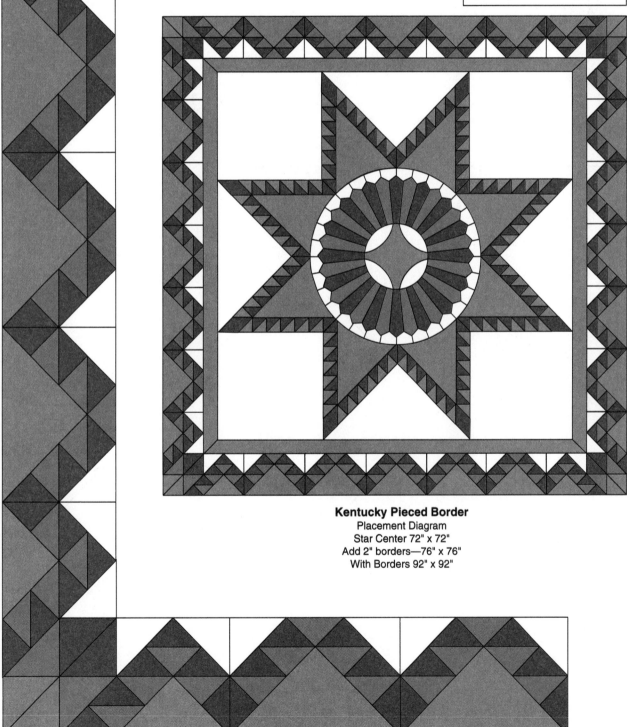

Kentucky Pieced Border
Placement Diagram
Star Center 72" x 72"
Add 2" borders—76" x 76"
With Borders 92" x 92"

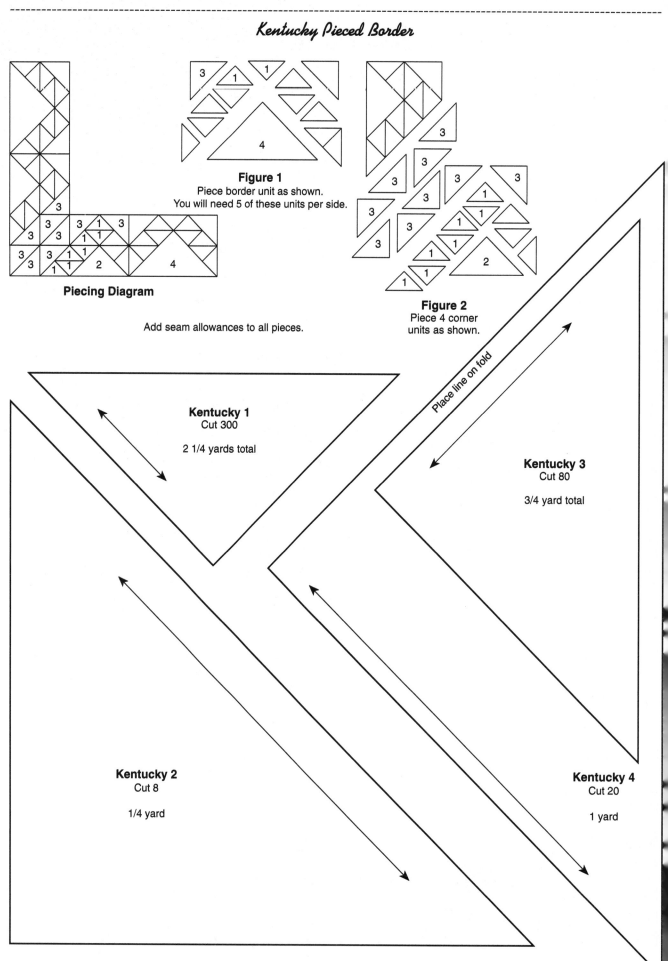

Figure 1
Piece border unit as shown.
You will need 5 of these units per side.

Piecing Diagram

Add seam allowances to all pieces.

Figure 2
Piece 4 corner
units as shown.

Place line on fold

Kentucky 1
Cut 300

2 1/4 yards total

Kentucky 3
Cut 80

3/4 yard total

Kentucky 2
Cut 8

1/4 yard

Kentucky 4
Cut 20

1 yard

Louisiana Pieced Border

Piecing this border is a snap! Even though there are more units per side, the units are easy to piece. Have fun using this border design on quilts having square pieces or triangles in the center.

Border Unit: 6" x 8"—12 per side
Corner Unit: 8" x 8"—4 corners

Border is shown with the star pattern for Royal Star of Louisiana. The pattern for the star is available in *Royal Stars of the States*, also published by House of White Birches. See ordering information on Page 159

Louisiana Pieced Border
Placement Diagram
Star Center 72" x 72"
With Borders 88" x 88"

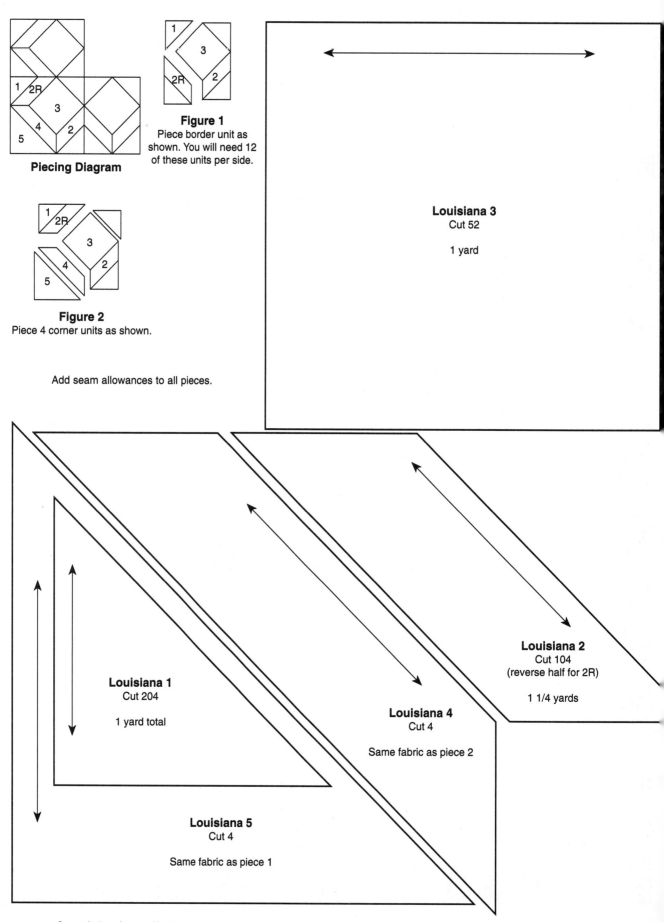

Piecing Diagram

Figure 1
Piece border unit as shown. You will need 12 of these units per side.

Figure 2
Piece 4 corner units as shown.

Add seam allowances to all pieces.

Louisiana 3
Cut 52

1 yard

Louisiana 2
Cut 104
(reverse half for 2R)

1 1/4 yards

Louisiana 1
Cut 204

1 yard total

Louisiana 4
Cut 4

Same fabric as piece 2

Louisiana 5
Cut 4

Same fabric as piece 1

Maine Pieced Border

The diamond shapes on this border design are quite large, making piecing the units quicker. The four-diamond star shape would make a good border addition for a variety of star patterns.

Border Units: 8" wide
Corner Unit: Irregular shape; 8" wide—4 corners

Border is shown with the star pattern for Royal Star of Maine. The pattern for the star is available in *Royal Stars of the States*, also published by House of White Birches. See ordering information on Page 159.

Maine Pieced Border
Placement Diagram
Star Center 75" x 75"
Add 1/2" borders—76" x 76"
With Borders 92" x 92"

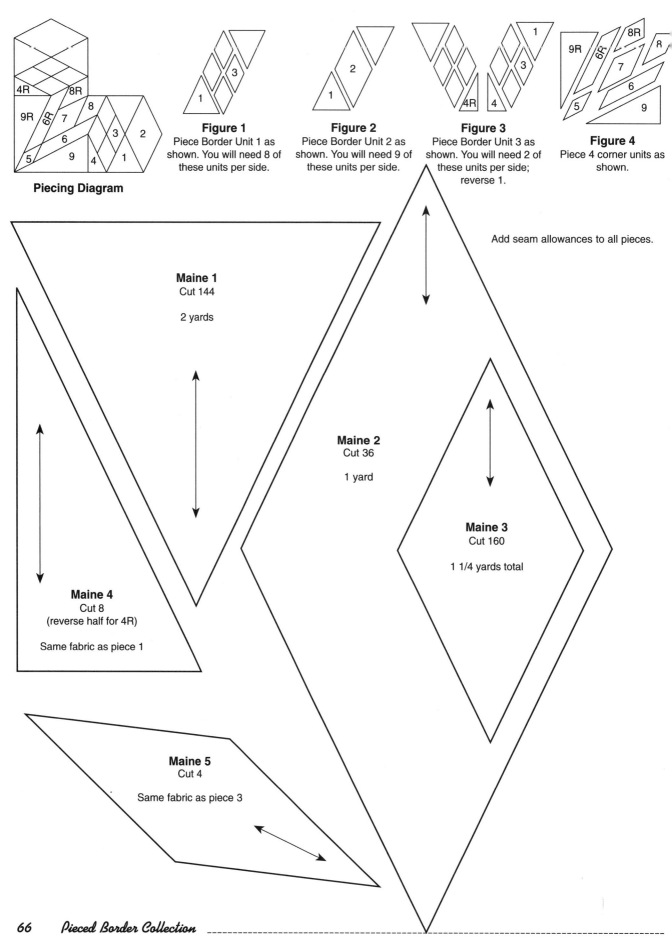

Piecing Diagram

Figure 1
Piece Border Unit 1 as shown. You will need 8 of these units per side.

Figure 2
Piece Border Unit 2 as shown. You will need 9 of these units per side.

Figure 3
Piece Border Unit 3 as shown. You will need 2 of these units per side; reverse 1.

Figure 4
Piece 4 corner units as shown.

Add seam allowances to all pieces.

Maine 1
Cut 144

2 yards

Maine 2
Cut 36

1 yard

Maine 3
Cut 160

1 1/4 yards total

Maine 4
Cut 8
(reverse half for 4R)

Same fabric as piece 1

Maine 5
Cut 4

Same fabric as piece 3

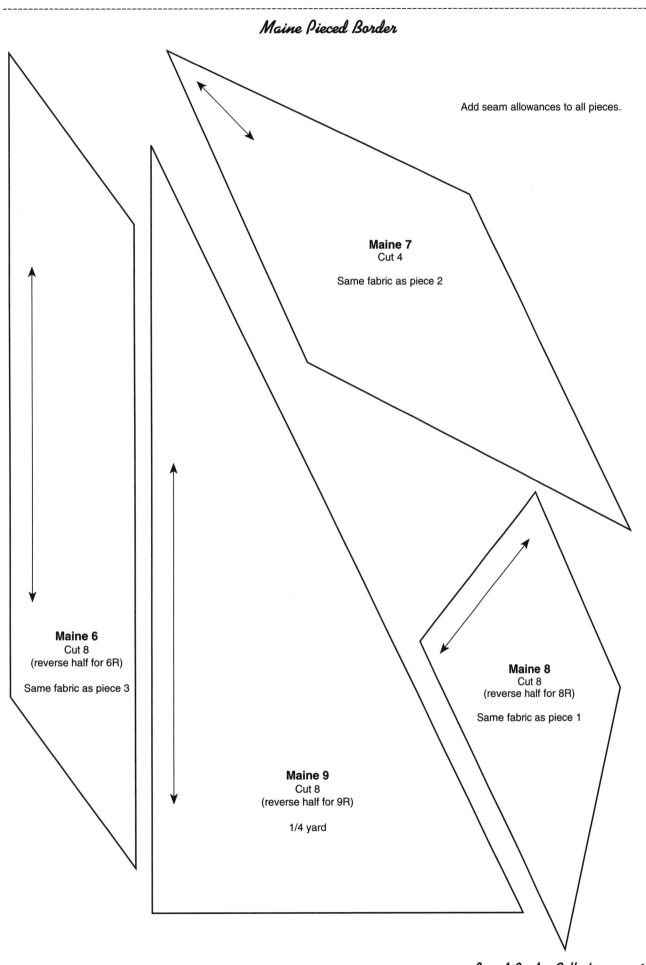

Add seam allowances to all pieces.

Maine 7
Cut 4

Same fabric as piece 2

Maine 6
Cut 8
(reverse half for 6R)

Same fabric as piece 3

Maine 8
Cut 8
(reverse half for 8R)

Same fabric as piece 1

Maine 9
Cut 8
(reverse half for 9R)

1/4 yard

Maryland Pieced Border

Here is yet another easy border to piece. Made up of large pieces in the outside border triangle unit and diamond pieces in the inside triangle, this border would work up quickly by machine. Because of its size, changing a quilt to fit it would be more difficult.

Border Unit: 7 1/2" x 15"—5 per side
Corner Unit: 7 1/2" x 7 1/2"—4 corners

Border is shown with the star pattern for Royal Star of Maryland. The pattern for the star is available in *Royal Stars of the States*, also published by House of White Birches. See ordering information on Page 159.

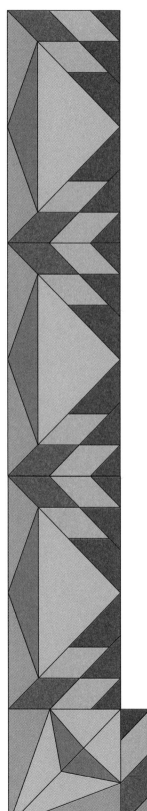

Maryland Pieced Border
Placement Diagram
Star Center 75" x 75"
With Borders 90" x 90"

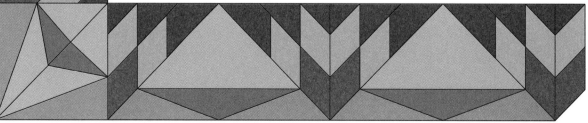

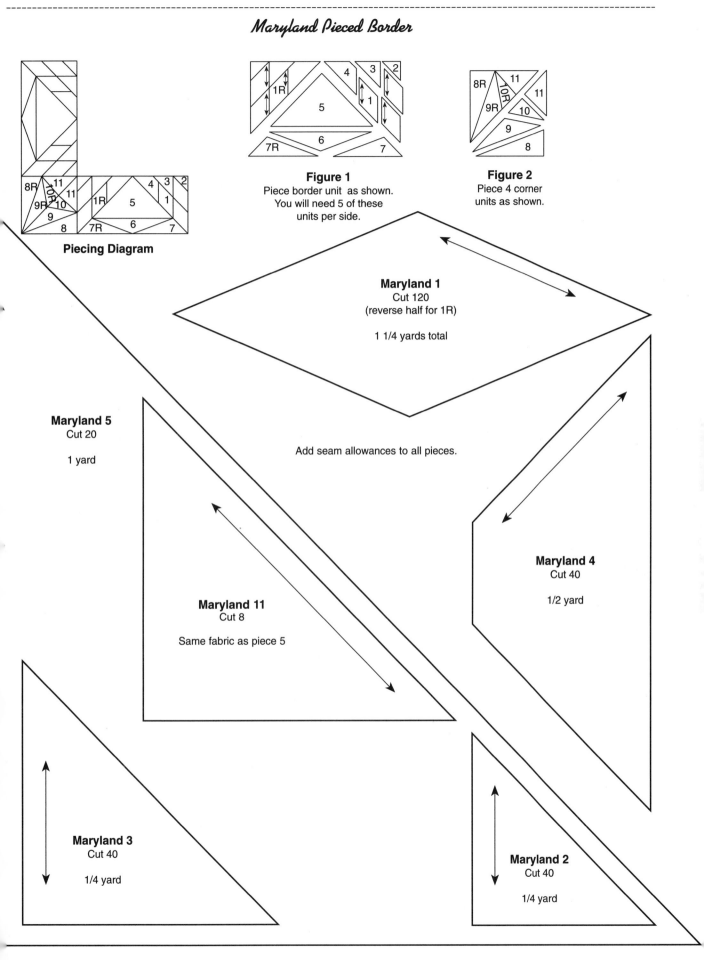

Figure 1
Piece border unit as shown.
You will need 5 of these
units per side.

Figure 2
Piece 4 corner
units as shown.

Piecing Diagram

Maryland 1
Cut 120
(reverse half for 1R)

1 1/4 yards total

Maryland 5
Cut 20

1 yard

Add seam allowances to all pieces.

Maryland 4
Cut 40

1/2 yard

Maryland 11
Cut 8

Same fabric as piece 5

Maryland 3
Cut 40

1/4 yard

Maryland 2
Cut 40

1/4 yard

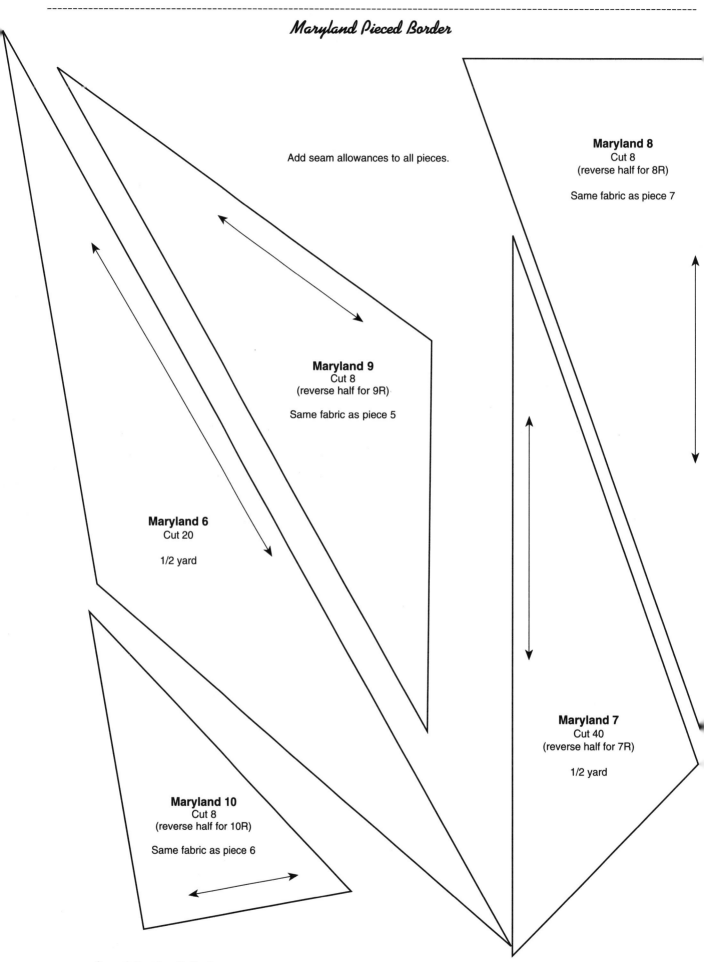

Add seam allowances to all pieces.

Maryland 8
Cut 8
(reverse half for 8R)

Same fabric as piece 7

Maryland 9
Cut 8
(reverse half for 9R)

Same fabric as piece 5

Maryland 6
Cut 20

1/2 yard

Maryland 7
Cut 40
(reverse half for 7R)

1/2 yard

Maryland 10
Cut 8
(reverse half for 10R)

Same fabric as piece 6

Massachusetts Pieced Border

In the original center star design, the diamond shape is stitched in rows with solid fabric strips between to make the points of the stars. In this border design, the diamonds are stitched in a strip of four but set on the diagonal.

Border Unit 1: 8" x 8"—8 per side
Border Unit 2: 2" x 8"—2 per side
Corner Unit: 8" x 9"—4 corners

Border is shown with the star pattern for Royal Star of Massachusetts. The pattern for the star is available in *Royal Stars of the States*, also published by House of White Birches. See ordering information on Page 159.

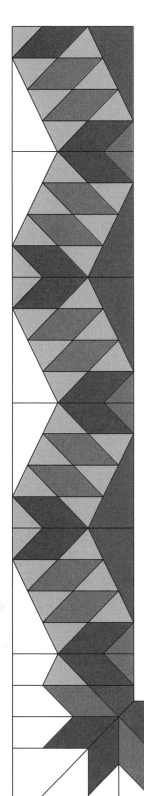

Massachusetts Pieced Border
Placement Diagram
Star Center 66" x 66"
Add 2" borders—70" x 70"
With Borders 86" x 86"

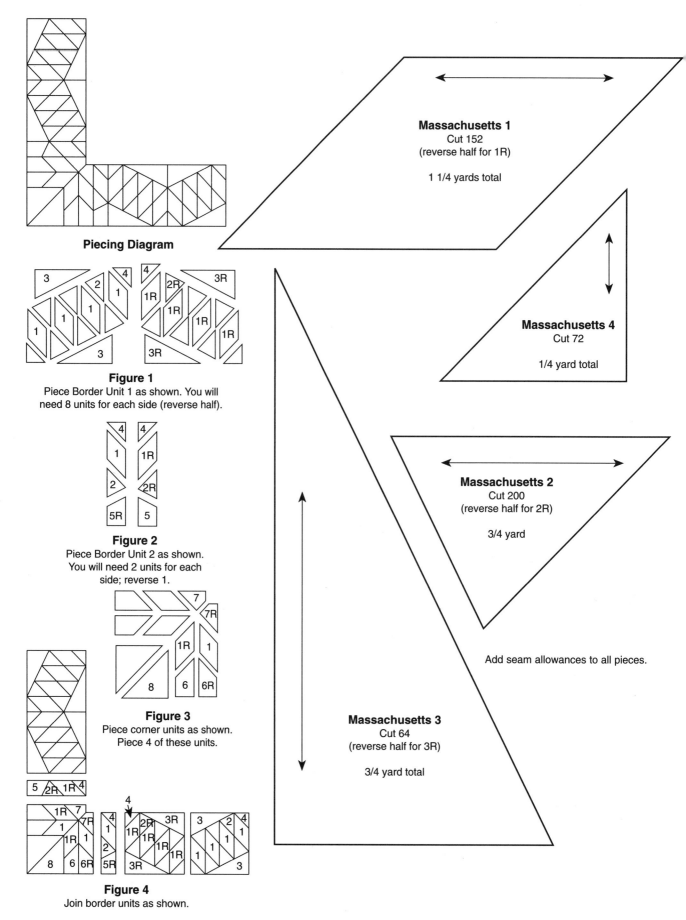

Piecing Diagram

Figure 1
Piece Border Unit 1 as shown. You will
need 8 units for each side (reverse half).

Figure 2
Piece Border Unit 2 as shown.
You will need 2 units for each
side; reverse 1.

Figure 3
Piece corner units as shown.
Piece 4 of these units.

Figure 4
Join border units as shown.

Massachusetts 1
Cut 152
(reverse half for 1R)

1 1/4 yards total

Massachusetts 4
Cut 72

1/4 yard total

Massachusetts 2
Cut 200
(reverse half for 2R)

3/4 yard

Add seam allowances to all pieces.

Massachusetts 3
Cut 64
(reverse half for 3R)

3/4 yard total

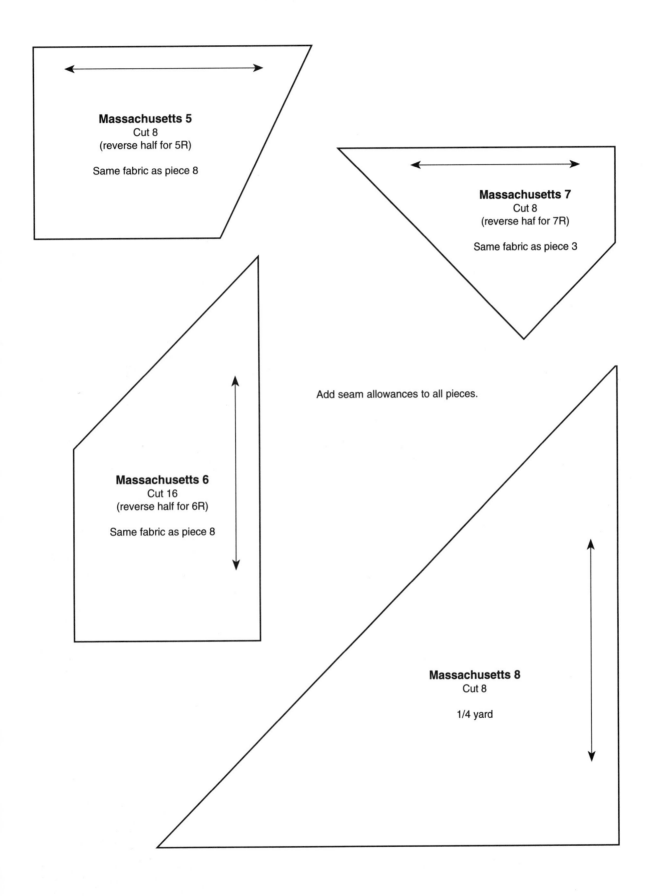

Massachusetts 5
Cut 8
(reverse half for 5R)

Same fabric as piece 8

Massachusetts 7
Cut 8
(reverse haf for 7R)

Same fabric as piece 3

Add seam allowances to all pieces.

Massachusetts 6
Cut 16
(reverse half for 6R)

Same fabric as piece 8

Massachusetts 8
Cut 8

1/4 yard

Michigan Pieced Border

Add this simple narrow border to the Michigan star or other quilts with similar diamond shapes. Change the position of the diamonds and face them toward the outside for a different look.

Border Unit: 5" x 16"—4 per side
Corner Unit: Irregular shape—4 corners

Border is shown with the star pattern for Royal Star of Michigan. The pattern for the star is available in *Royal Stars of the States*, also published by House of White Birches. See ordering information on Page 159.

Michigan Pieced Border
Placement Diagram
Star Center 66 1/2" x 66 1/2"
Add 8 3/4" borders—84" x 84"
With Borders 94" x 94"

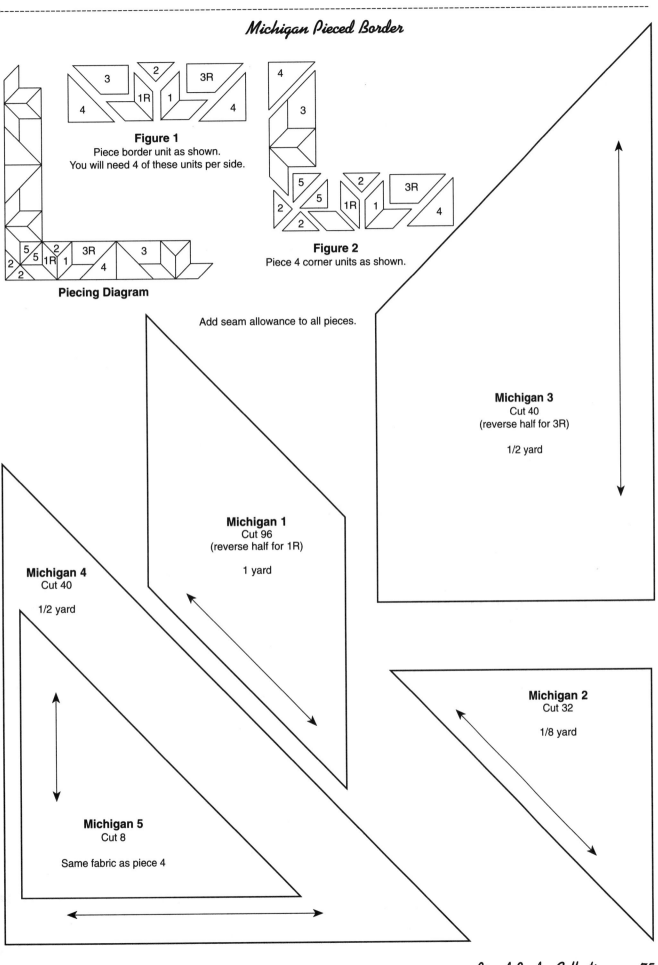

Figure 1
Piece border unit as shown.
You will need 4 of these units per side.

Piecing Diagram

Figure 2
Piece 4 corner units as shown.

Add seam allowance to all pieces.

Michigan 3
Cut 40
(reverse half for 3R)

1/2 yard

Michigan 1
Cut 96
(reverse half for 1R)

1 yard

Michigan 4
Cut 40

1/2 yard

Michigan 2
Cut 32

1/8 yard

Michigan 5
Cut 8

Same fabric as piece 4

Minnesota Pieced Border

This unusual border design looks like a man's vest and tie if you look at it along the bottom of the drawing. The V-shaped pieces repeat the design from the center of the Royal Star of Minnesota shown in the large drawing. Change the dark and light colors around to focus your eye on different pieces in the border until you have found your favorite version.

Border Unit 1: 10" x 10"—6 per side
Border Unit 2: Irregular shape; 10" wide—2 per side
Corner Unit: 8 1/2" x 8 1/2"—4 corners

Border is shown with the star pattern for Royal Star of Minnesota. The pattern for the star is available in *Royal Stars of the States*, also published by House of White Birches. See ordering information on Page 159.

Minnesota Pieced Border
Placement Diagram
Star Center 75" x 75"
With Borders 95" x 95"

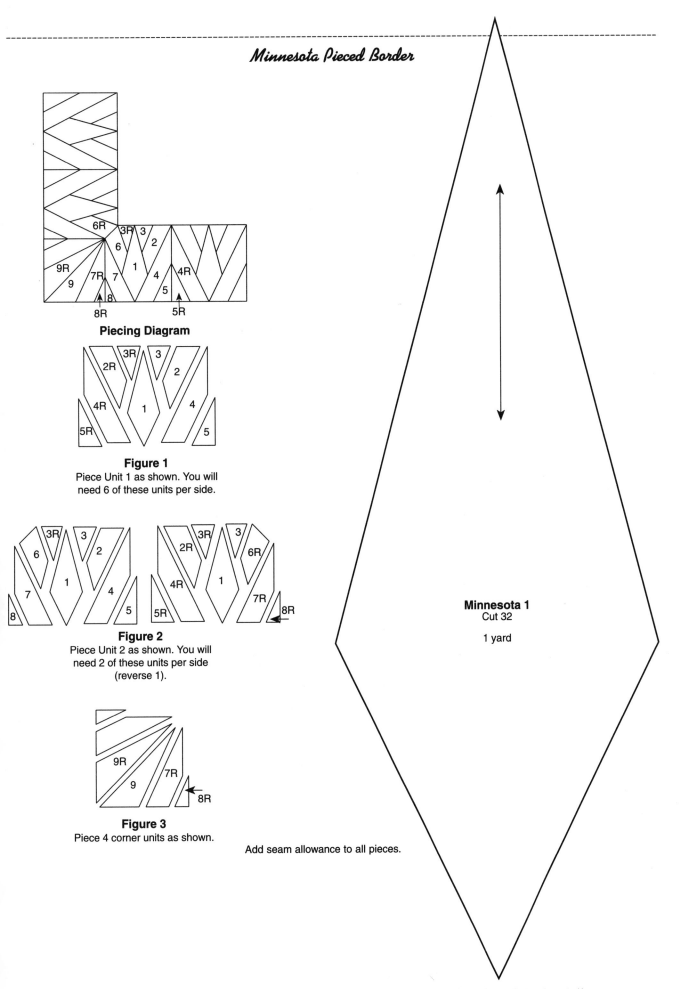

Piecing Diagram

Figure 1
Piece Unit 1 as shown. You will
need 6 of these units per side.

Figure 2
Piece Unit 2 as shown. You will
need 2 of these units per side
(reverse 1).

Figure 3
Piece 4 corner units as shown.

Add seam allowance to all pieces.

Minnesota 1
Cut 32

1 yard

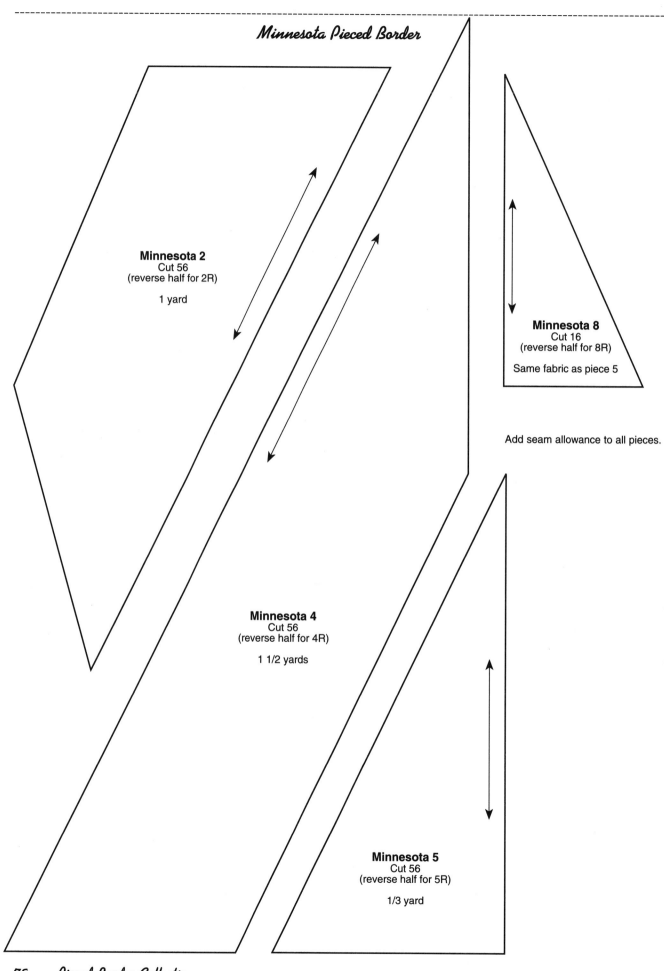

Minnesota 2
Cut 56
(reverse half for 2R)

1 yard

Minnesota 8
Cut 16
(reverse half for 8R)

Same fabric as piece 5

Add seam allowance to all pieces.

Minnesota 4
Cut 56
(reverse half for 4R)

1 1/2 yards

Minnesota 5
Cut 56
(reverse half for 5R)

1/3 yard

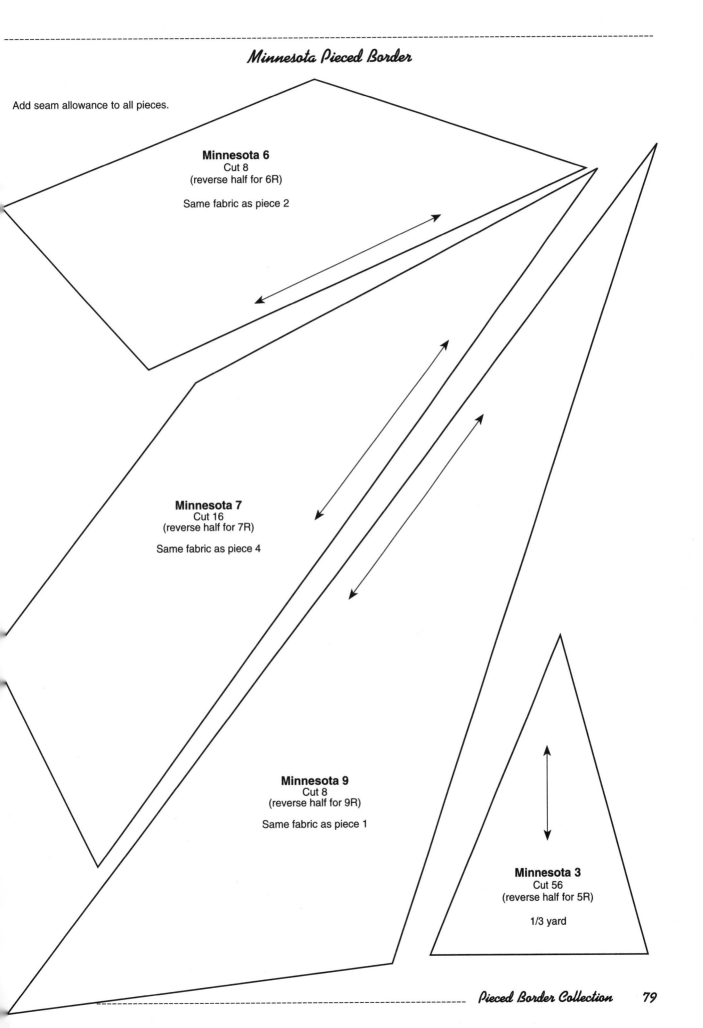

Add seam allowance to all pieces.

Minnesota 6
Cut 8
(reverse half for 6R)

Same fabric as piece 2

Minnesota 7
Cut 16
(reverse half for 7R)

Same fabric as piece 4

Minnesota 9
Cut 8
(reverse half for 9R)

Same fabric as piece 1

Minnesota 3
Cut 56
(reverse half for 5R)

1/3 yard

Mississippi Pieced Border

The large strips used on this border make it easy to piece. Use one color from the center to accent corners and center sections as shown in the colored drawing.

Border Unit 1: Irregular shape; 6" wide—2 per side
Border Unit 2: Irregular shape; 6" wide—1 per side
Border Unit 3: Diamond shape; 6" wide—4 per side

Border is shown with the star pattern for Royal Star of Mississippi. The pattern for the star is available in *Royal Stars of the States*, also published by House of White Birches. See ordering information on Page 159.

Mississippi Pieced Border
Placement Diagram
Star Center 75" x 75"
With Borders 87" x 87"

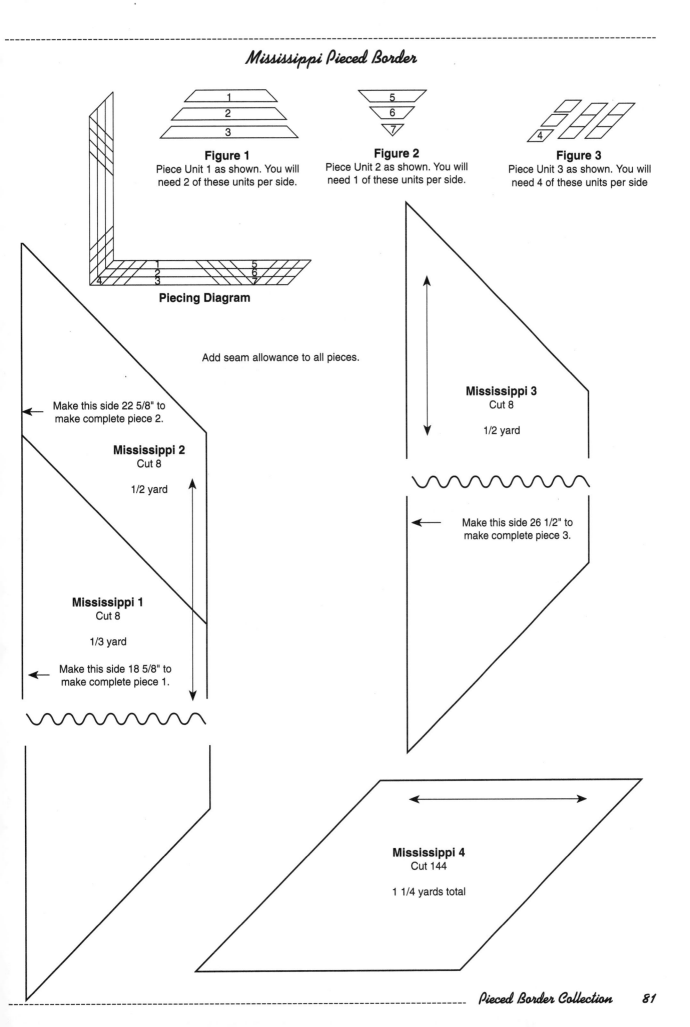

Figure 1
Piece Unit 1 as shown. You will
need 2 of these units per side.

Figure 2
Piece Unit 2 as shown. You will
need 1 of these units per side.

Figure 3
Piece Unit 3 as shown. You will
need 4 of these units per side

Piecing Diagram

Add seam allowance to all pieces.

Make this side 22 5/8" to
make complete piece 2.

Mississippi 2
Cut 8

1/2 yard

Mississippi 3
Cut 8

1/2 yard

Mississippi 1
Cut 8

1/3 yard

Make this side 18 5/8" to
make complete piece 1.

Make this side 26 1/2" to
make complete piece 3.

Mississippi 4
Cut 144

1 1/4 yards total

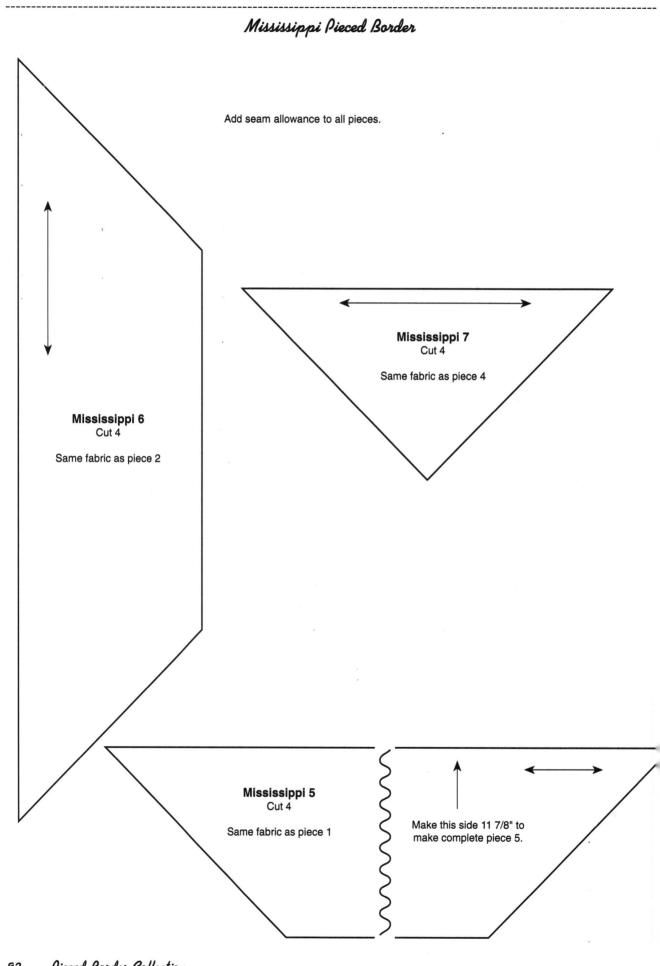

Add seam allowance to all pieces.

Mississippi 7
Cut 4

Same fabric as piece 4

Mississippi 6
Cut 4

Same fabric as piece 2

Mississippi 5
Cut 4

Same fabric as piece 1

Make this side 11 7/8" to
make complete piece 5.

Missouri Pieced Border

This border is pieced in rows instead of units. Because of this, it could be made with scraps and used on any scrap quilt with triangle shapes in the center pieced section. Here the color arrangement is coordinated with the center design in a planned arrangement. Either way, it is easy to piece.

Border Pieced in Rows: 7" wide
Note: Piece this border design in rows, setting on corner pieces referring to the Figure drawings and the Placement Diagram.

Border is shown with the star pattern for Royal Star of Missouri. The pattern for the star is available in *Royal Stars of the States*, also published by House of White Birches. See ordering information on Page 159

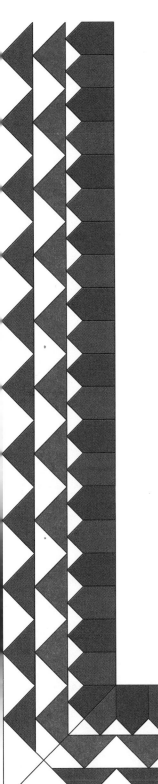

Missouri Pieced Border
Placement Diagram
Star Center 72" x 72"
With Borders 86" x 86"

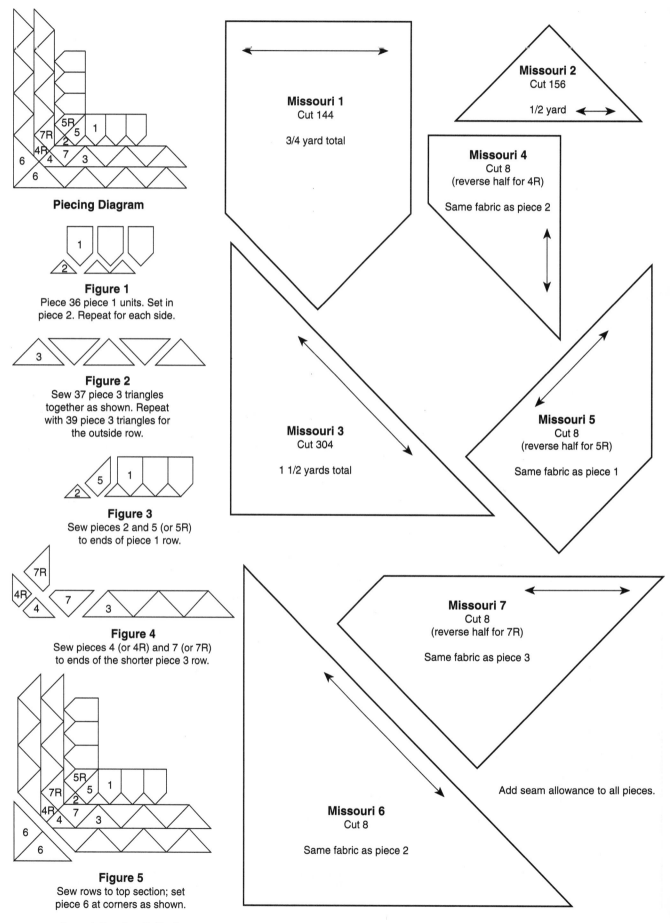

Piecing Diagram

Figure 1
Piece 36 piece 1 units. Set in
piece 2. Repeat for each side.

Figure 2
Sew 37 piece 3 triangles
together as shown. Repeat
with 39 piece 3 triangles for
the outside row.

Figure 3
Sew pieces 2 and 5 (or 5R)
to ends of piece 1 row.

Figure 4
Sew pieces 4 (or 4R) and 7 (or 7R)
to ends of the shorter piece 3 row.

Figure 5
Sew rows to top section; set
piece 6 at corners as shown.

Missouri 1
Cut 144

3/4 yard total

Missouri 2
Cut 156

1/2 yard

Missouri 4
Cut 8
(reverse half for 4R)

Same fabric as piece 2

Missouri 3
Cut 304

1 1/2 yards total

Missouri 5
Cut 8
(reverse half for 5R)

Same fabric as piece 1

Missouri 7
Cut 8
(reverse half for 7R)

Same fabric as piece 3

Add seam allowance to all pieces.

Missouri 6
Cut 8

Same fabric as piece 2

Montana Pieced Border

Although this border design repeats the shape of the star pattern it was designed for, it could be used on any design with similar shapes. The Eight-Pointed Star blocks in the corners make it a useful design for any quilt using a star shape.

Border Unit: 8" x 9 1/2"—9 per side
Corner Unit: 9 1/2" x 9 1/2"—4 corners

Border is shown with the star pattern for Royal Star of Montana. The pattern for the star is available in *Royal Stars of the States*, also published by House of White Birches. See ordering information on Page 159.

Montana Pieced Border
Placement Diagram
Star Center 72" x 72"
With Borders 91" x 91"

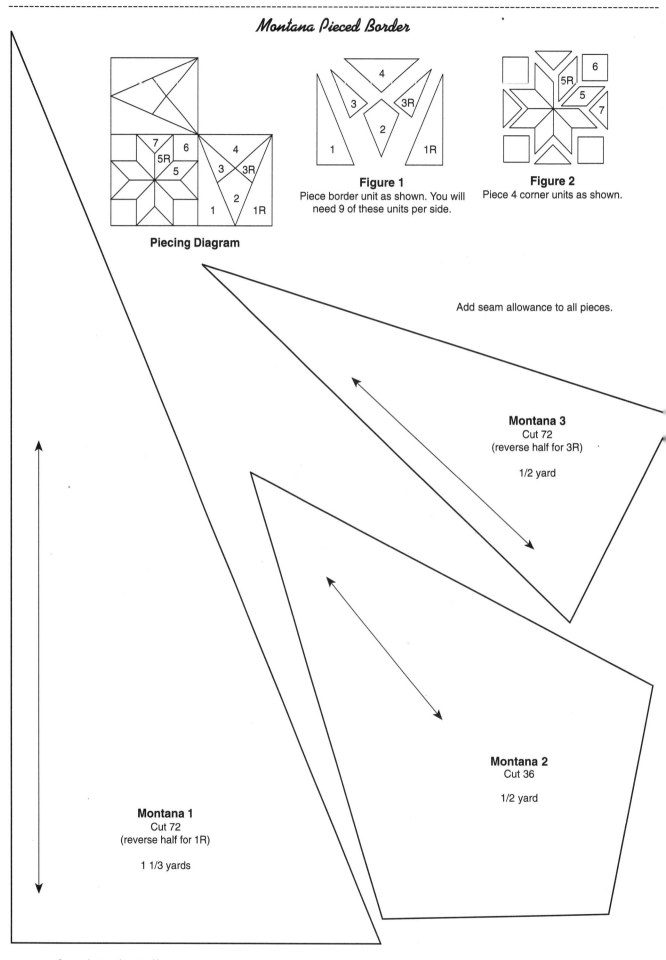

Piecing Diagram

Figure 1
Piece border unit as shown. You will
need 9 of these units per side.

Figure 2
Piece 4 corner units as shown.

Add seam allowance to all pieces.

Montana 3
Cut 72
(reverse half for 3R)

1/2 yard

Montana 2
Cut 36

1/2 yard

Montana 1
Cut 72
(reverse half for 1R)

1 1/3 yards

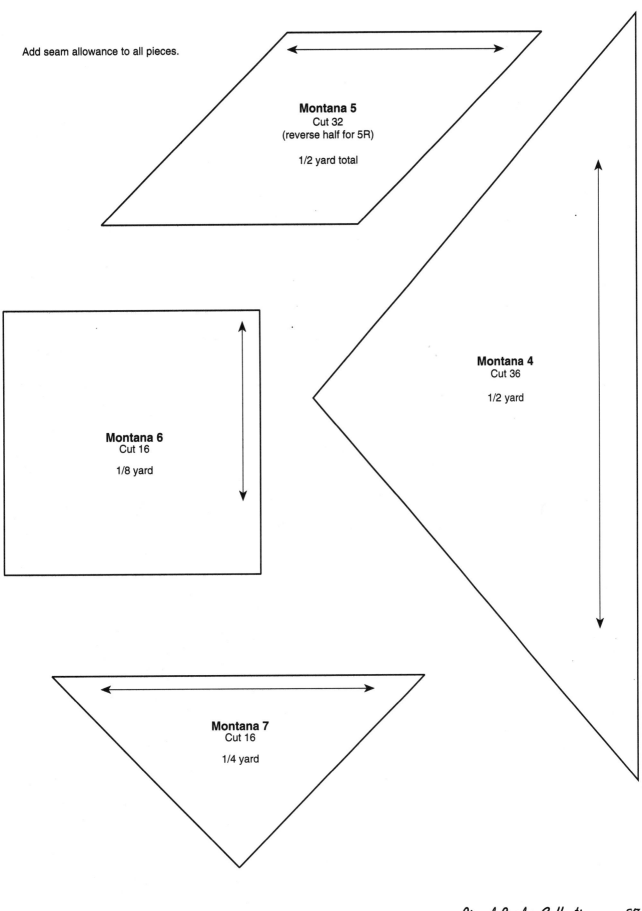

Add seam allowance to all pieces.

Montana 5
Cut 32
(reverse half for 5R)

1/2 yard total

Montana 4
Cut 36

1/2 yard

Montana 6
Cut 16

1/8 yard

Montana 7
Cut 16

1/4 yard

Nebraska Pieced Border

Make this pieced border using bold colors to accent the wing-shaped pieces. The combination of red and black shown in the drawing compares to colors used in Amish quilts.

Border Unit: 6" x 8"—12 per side
Corner Unit: Irregular shape—4 corners

Border is shown with the star pattern for Royal Star of Nebraska. The pattern for the star is available in *Royal Stars of the States*, also published by House of White Birches. See ordering information on Page 159.

Nebraska Pieced Border
Placement Diagram
Star Center 72" x 72"
Add 3" borders—78" x 78"
With Borders 94" x 94"

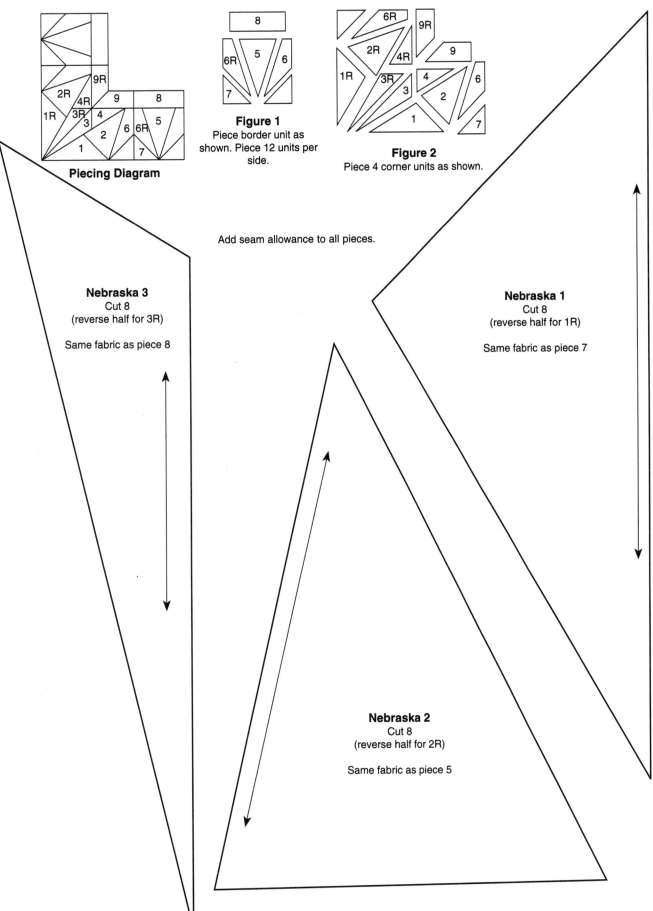

Piecing Diagram

Figure 1
Piece border unit as shown. Piece 12 units per side.

Figure 2
Piece 4 corner units as shown.

Add seam allowance to all pieces.

Nebraska 3
Cut 8
(reverse half for 3R)

Same fabric as piece 8

Nebraska 1
Cut 8
(reverse half for 1R)

Same fabric as piece 7

Nebraska 2
Cut 8
(reverse half for 2R)

Same fabric as piece 5

Add seam allowance to all pieces.

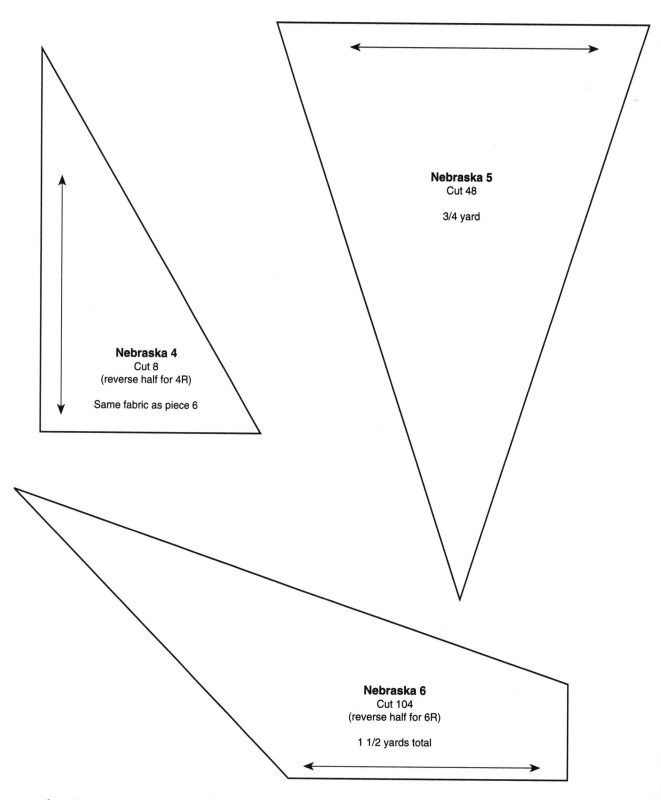

Nebraska 5
Cut 48

3/4 yard

Nebraska 4
Cut 8
(reverse half for 4R)

Same fabric as piece 6

Nebraska 6
Cut 104
(reverse half for 6R)

1 1/2 yards total

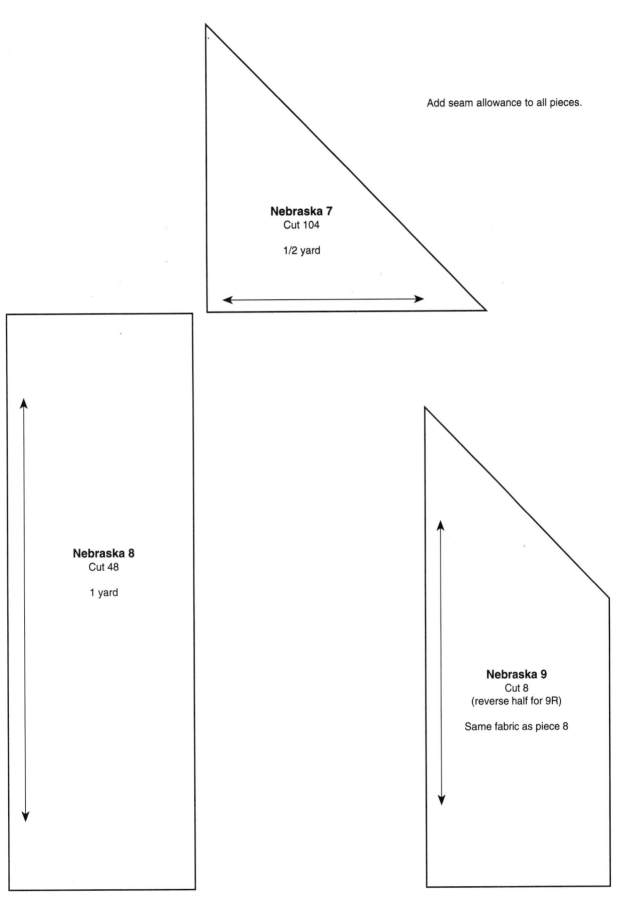

Add seam allowance to all pieces.

Nebraska 7
Cut 104

1/2 yard

Nebraska 8
Cut 48

1 yard

Nebraska 9
Cut 8
(reverse half for 9R)

Same fabric as piece 8

Nevada Pieced Border

This simple diamond border can be used on almost any quilt. Make the border with only two fabrics as shown or with scraps. Piecing will take some time, but the result is a spectacular frame for your quilt.

Border Unit 1: Irregular shape; 9" wide—36 per side
Border Unit 2: Triangular shape—9" wide—1 per side

Border is shown with the star pattern for Royal Star of Nevada. The pattern for the star is available in *Royal Stars of the States*, also published by House of White Birches. See ordering information on Page 159.

Nevada Pieced Border
Placement Diagram
Star Center 72" x 72"
With Borders 90" x 90"

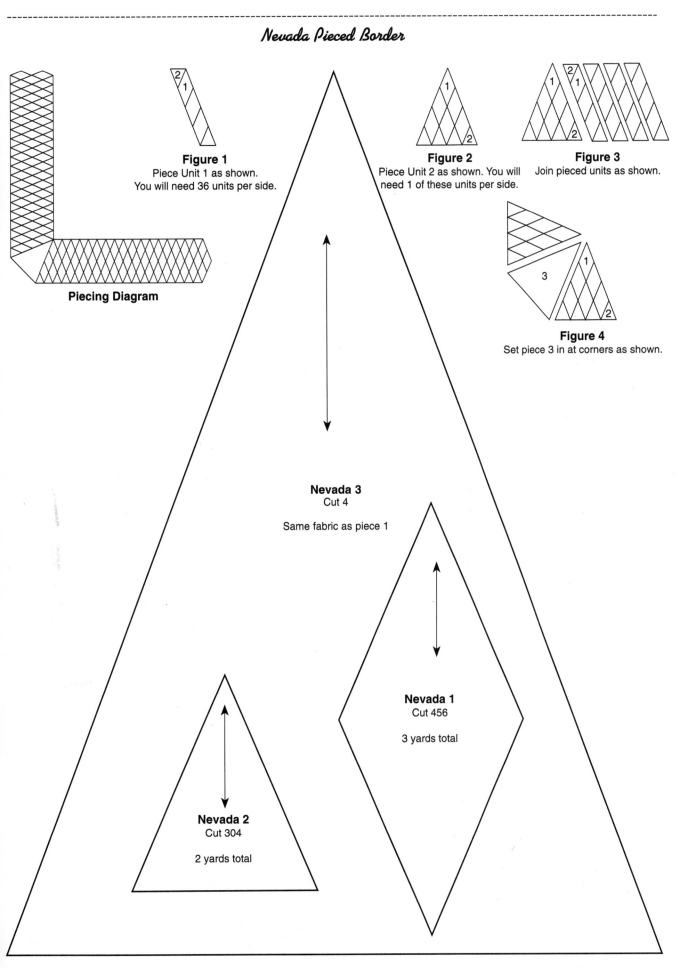

Figure 1
Piece Unit 1 as shown.
You will need 36 units per side.

Figure 2
Piece Unit 2 as shown. You will
need 1 of these units per side.

Figure 3
Join pieced units as shown.

Piecing Diagram

Figure 4
Set piece 3 in at corners as shown.

Nevada 3
Cut 4

Same fabric as piece 1

Nevada 1
Cut 456

3 yards total

Nevada 2
Cut 304

2 yards total

New Hampshire Pieced Border

Only three units make up the New Hampshire border design. Because the pieces are large, they are very easy to piece.

Border Unit 1: Irregular shape—10" wide
Border Unit 2: Irregular shape—10" wide
Corner Unit: Irregular shape—10" wide

Border is shown with the star pattern for Royal Star of New Hampshire. The pattern for the star is available in *Royal Stars of the States*, also published by House of White Birches. See ordering information on Page 159.

New Hampshire Pieced Border
Placement Diagram
Star Center 72" x 72"
With Borders 92" x 92"

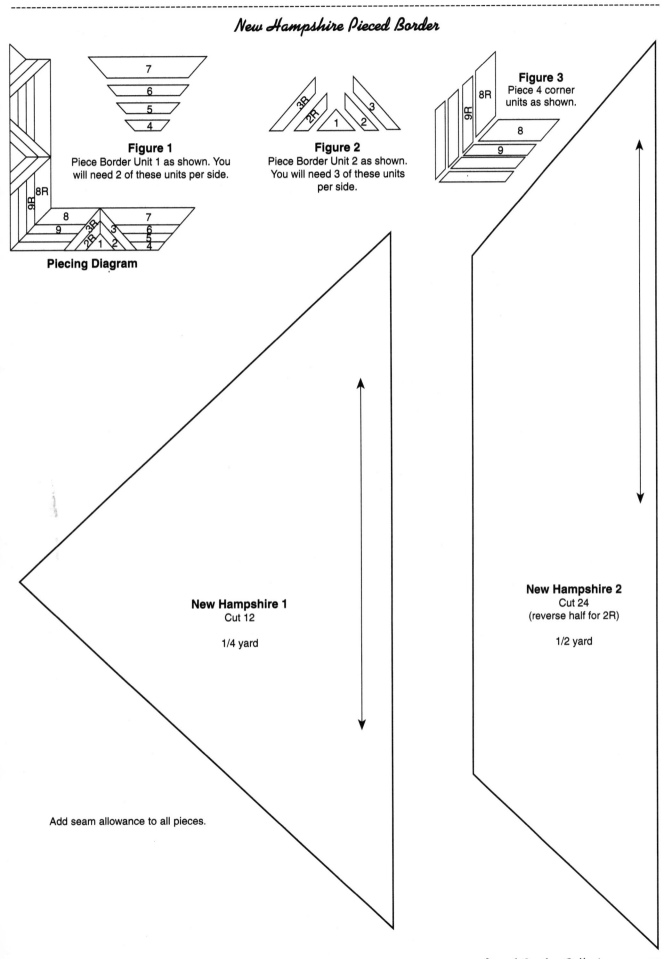

Figure 1
Piece Border Unit 1 as shown. You
will need 2 of these units per side.

Figure 2
Piece Border Unit 2 as shown.
You will need 3 of these units
per side.

Figure 3
Piece 4 corner
units as shown.

Piecing Diagram

New Hampshire 1
Cut 12

1/4 yard

New Hampshire 2
Cut 24
(reverse half for 2R)

1/2 yard

Add seam allowance to all pieces.

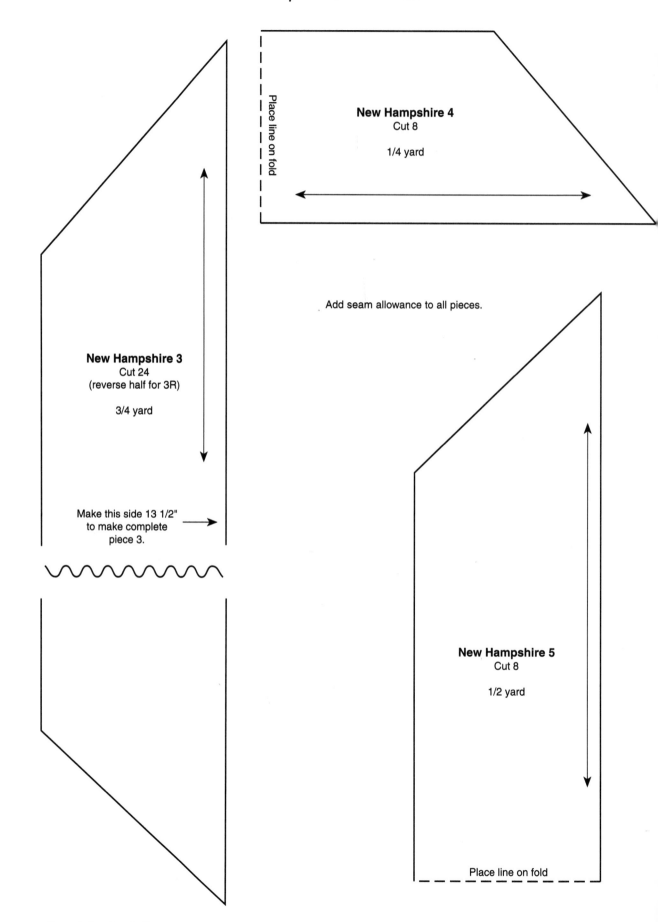

New Hampshire 4
Cut 8

1/4 yard

Place line on fold

Add seam allowance to all pieces.

New Hampshire 3
Cut 24
(reverse half for 3R)

3/4 yard

Make this side 13 1/2"
to make complete
piece 3.

New Hampshire 5
Cut 8

1/2 yard

Place line on fold

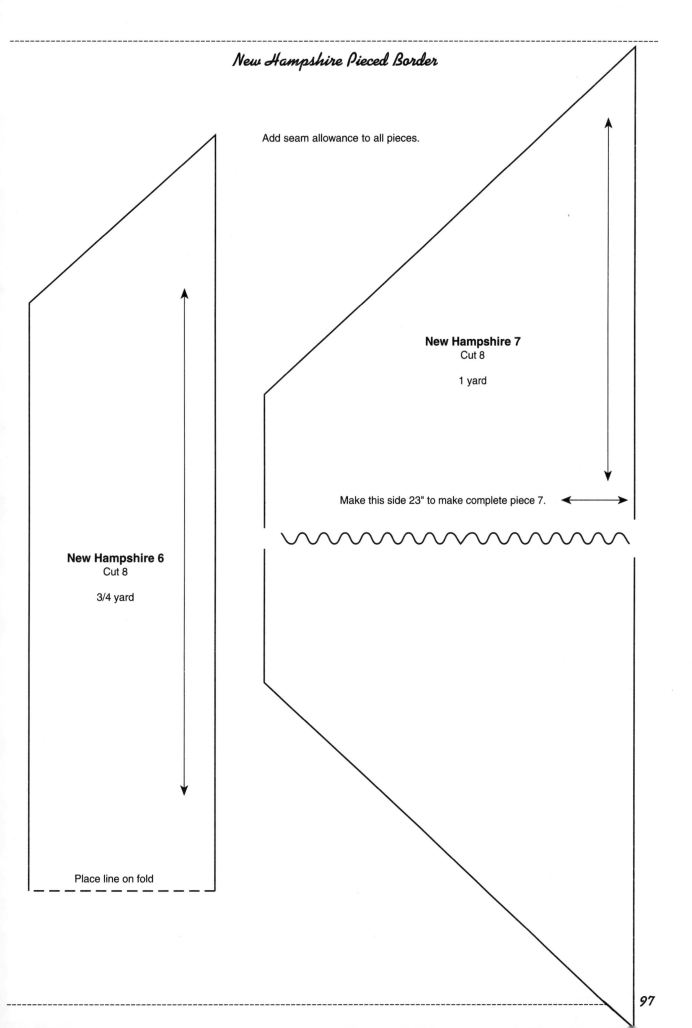

Add seam allowance to all pieces.

New Hampshire 7
Cut 8

1 yard

Make this side 23" to make complete piece 7.

New Hampshire 6
Cut 8

3/4 yard

Place line on fold

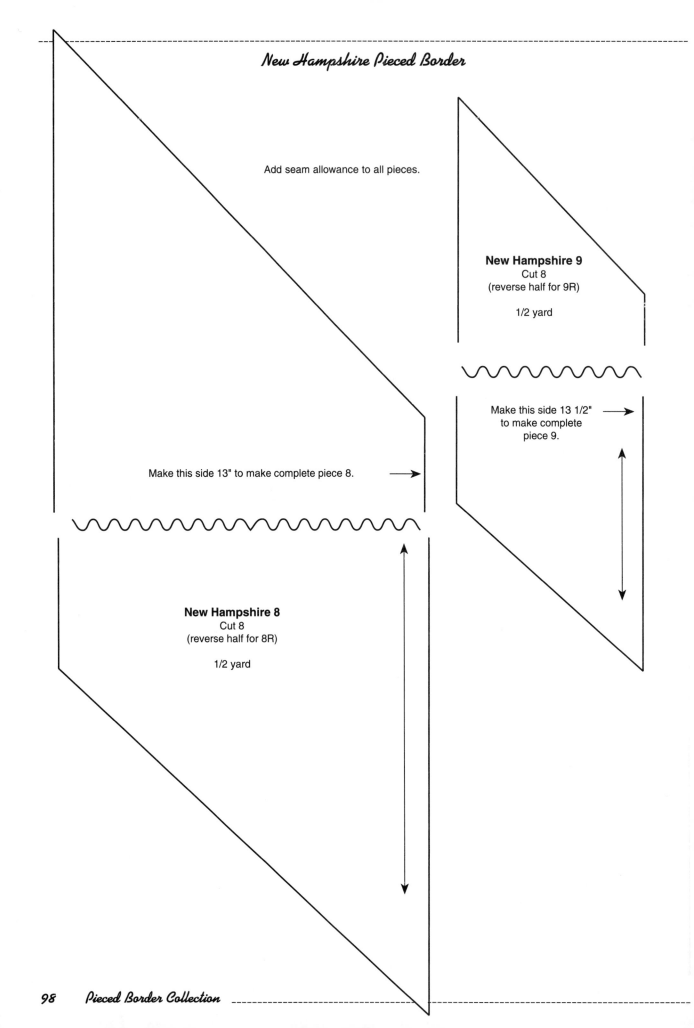

Add seam allowance to all pieces.

New Hampshire 9
Cut 8
(reverse half for 9R)

1/2 yard

Make this side 13 1/2"
to make complete
piece 9.

Make this side 13" to make complete piece 8.

New Hampshire 8
Cut 8
(reverse half for 8R)

1/2 yard

New Jersey Pieced Border

The side units on this pieced border design would be easy to strip-piece. If you sew one light and two dark fabric strips together and cut on an angle using the angle on piece 2 as a guide, you would save time cutting and piecing individual pieces. You could make a template combining three piece 2s to make cutting the strips accurate and easy.

Border Unit: 7 3/4" x 9 3/16" unit—10 per side
Corner Unit: 9 3/16" x 9 3/16"—4 corners

Border is shown with the star pattern for Royal Star of New Jersey. The pattern for the star is available in *Royal Stars of the States*, also published by House of White Birches. See ordering information on Page 159.

New Jersey Pieced Border
Placement Diagram
Star Center 75" x 75"
Add 1 1/4" borders—77 1/2" x 77 1/2"
With Borders 95 7/8" x 95 7/8"

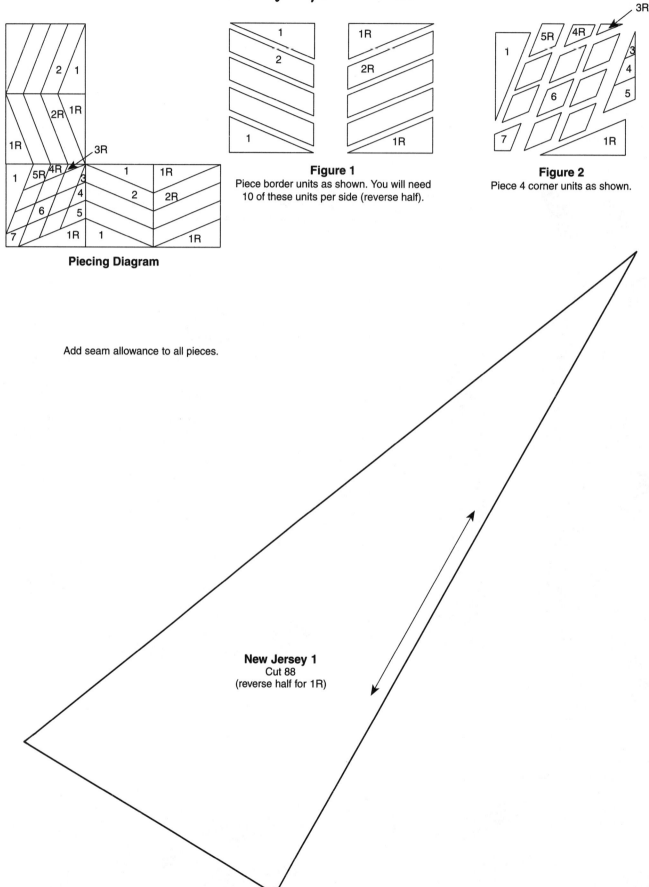

Piecing Diagram

Figure 1
Piece border units as shown. You will need
10 of these units per side (reverse half).

Figure 2
Piece 4 corner units as shown.

Add seam allowance to all pieces.

New Jersey 1
Cut 88
(reverse half for 1R)

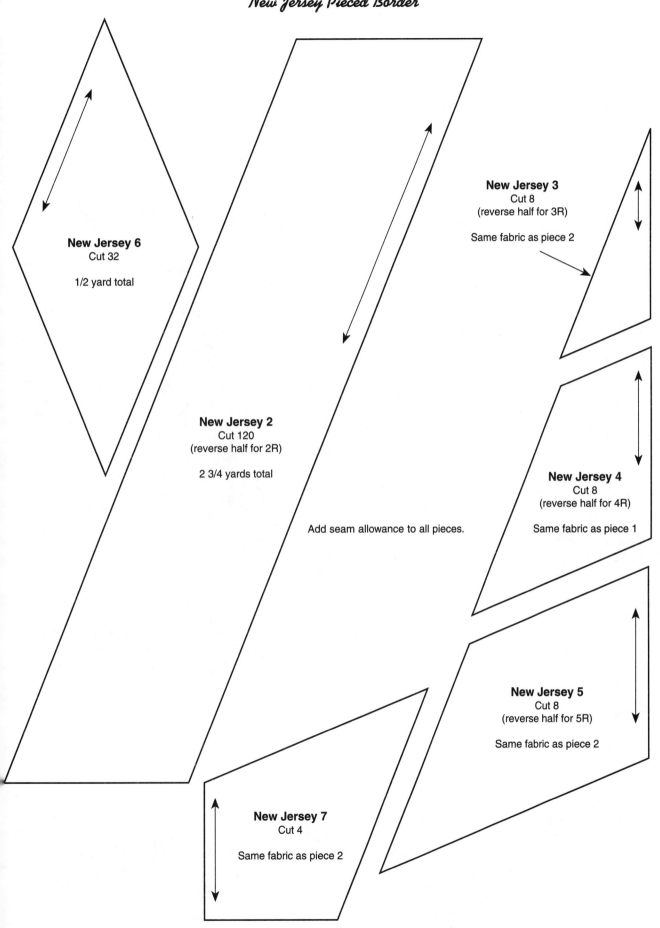

New Jersey 6
Cut 32

1/2 yard total

New Jersey 3
Cut 8
(reverse half for 3R)

Same fabric as piece 2

New Jersey 2
Cut 120
(reverse half for 2R)

2 3/4 yards total

Add seam allowance to all pieces.

New Jersey 4
Cut 8
(reverse half for 4R)

Same fabric as piece 1

New Jersey 5
Cut 8
(reverse half for 5R)

Same fabric as piece 2

New Jersey 7
Cut 4

Same fabric as piece 2

New Mexico Pieced Border

Although there are many pieces making up this border design, they are not difficult to piece. To avoid confusion, sew one unit at a time.

Border Unit: 10 1/4" x 12 3/4"—6 per side
Corner Unit: 10 1/4" x 10 1/4"—4 corners

Border is shown with the star pattern for Royal Star of New Mexico. The pattern for the star is available in *Royal Stars of the States*, also published by House of White Birches. See ordering information on Page 159.

New Mexico Pieced Border
Placement Diagram
Star Center 75" x 75"
Add 3/4" borders—76 1/2" x 76 1/2"
With Borders 97" x 97"

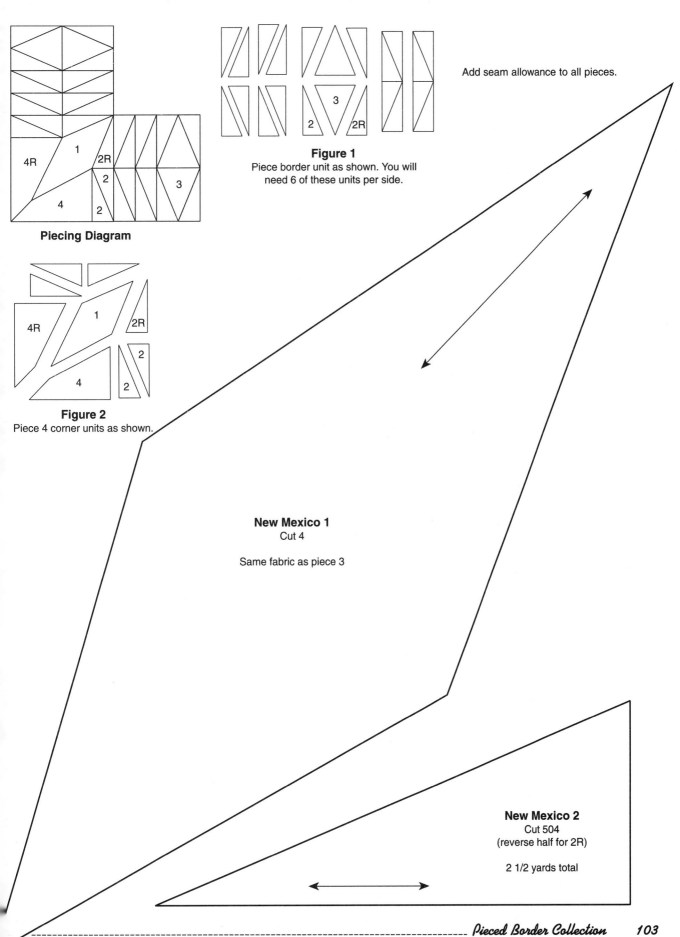

Piecing Diagram

Figure 1
Piece border unit as shown. You will
need 6 of these units per side.

Add seam allowance to all pieces.

Figure 2
Piece 4 corner units as shown.

New Mexico 1
Cut 4

Same fabric as piece 3

New Mexico 2
Cut 504
(reverse half for 2R)

2 1/2 yards total

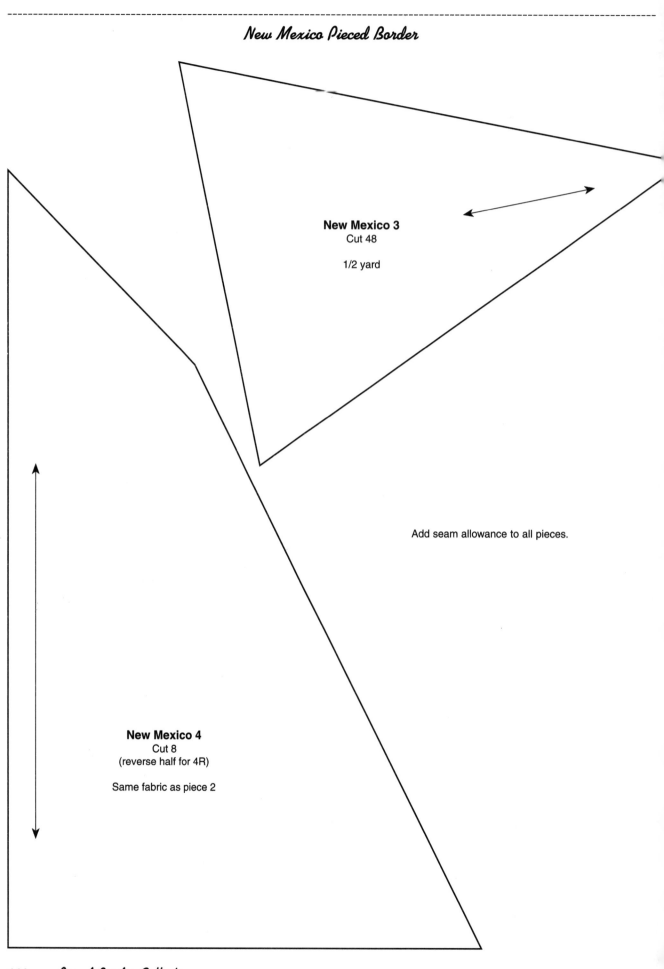

New Mexico 3
Cut 48

1/2 yard

Add seam allowance to all pieces.

New Mexico 4
Cut 8
(reverse half for 4R)

Same fabric as piece 2

New York Pieced Border

The fan shape from the center of the Royal Star of New York design has been repeated at the corners of this pieced border pattern. The color repetition combined with the shape repetition makes this a well-balanced quilt.

Border Unit 1: 6" x 9"—11 per side
Border Unit 2: 3" x 9"—2 per side
Corner Unit: Irregular shape; 9" wide—4 corners

Border is shown with the star pattern for Royal Star of New York. The pattern for the star is available in *Royal Stars of the States*, also published by House of White Birches. See ordering information on Page 159.

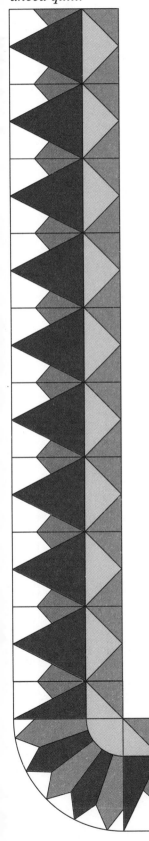

New York Pieced Border
Placement Diagram
Star Center 72" x 72"
With Borders 90" x 90"

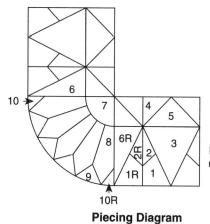

Piecing Diagram

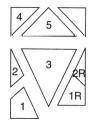

Figure 1
Piece Unit 1 as shown. You will need 11 of these units per side.

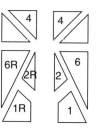

Figure 2
Piece Unit 2 as shown. You will need 2 of these units per side (reverse 1).

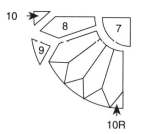

Figure 3
Piece 4 corner units as show

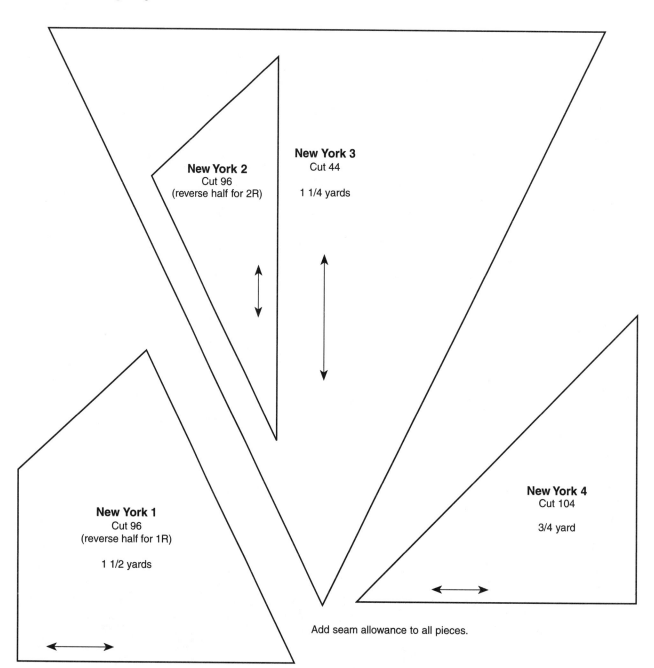

New York 2
Cut 96
(reverse half for 2R)

New York 3
Cut 44

1 1/4 yards

New York 1
Cut 96
(reverse half for 1R)

1 1/2 yards

New York 4
Cut 104

3/4 yard

Add seam allowance to all pieces.

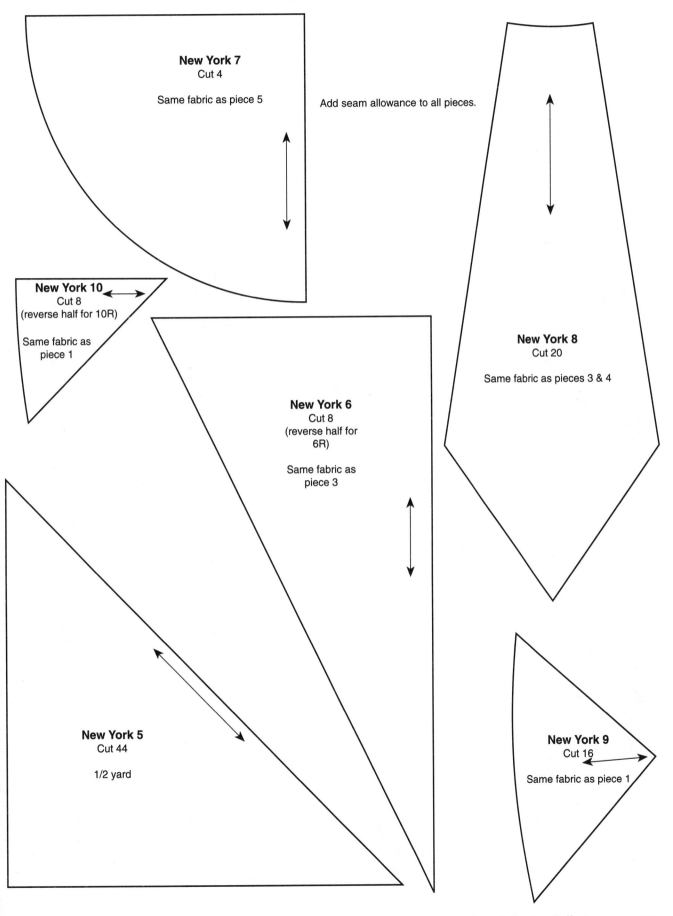

New York 7
Cut 4

Same fabric as piece 5

Add seam allowance to all pieces.

New York 10
Cut 8
(reverse half for 10R)

Same fabric as
piece 1

New York 6
Cut 8
(reverse half for
6R)

Same fabric as
piece 3

New York 8
Cut 20

Same fabric as pieces 3 & 4

New York 5
Cut 44

1/2 yard

New York 9
Cut 16

Same fabric as piece 1

North Carolina Pieced Border

The 8" blocks used for this pieced border all use the same pieces. Each block has two mirror-image sides using reversed pieces. Be careful piecing these very angled points.

Border Unit: 8" x 8"—10 per side
Corner Unit: 8" x 8"—4 corners (same as border unit)

Border is shown with the star pattern for Royal Star of North Carolina. The pattern for the star is available in *Royal Stars of the States*, also published by House of White Birches. See ordering information on Page 159.

North Carolina Pieced Border
Placement Diagram
Star Center 75" x 75"
Add 2 1/2" borders—80" x 80"
With Borders 96" x 96"

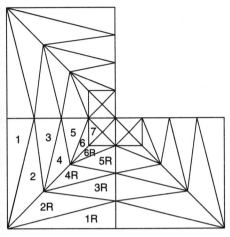

Piecing Diagram

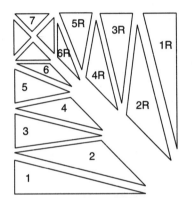

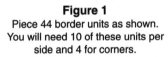

Figure 1
Piece 44 border units as shown.
You will need 10 of these units per
side and 4 for corners.

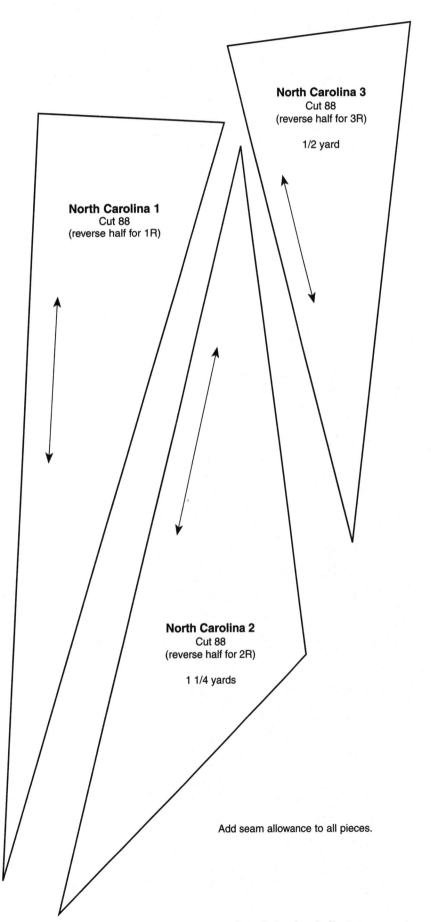

North Carolina 3
Cut 88
(reverse half for 3R)

1/2 yard

North Carolina 1
Cut 88
(reverse half for 1R)

North Carolina 2
Cut 88
(reverse half for 2R)

1 1/4 yards

Add seam allowance to all pieces.

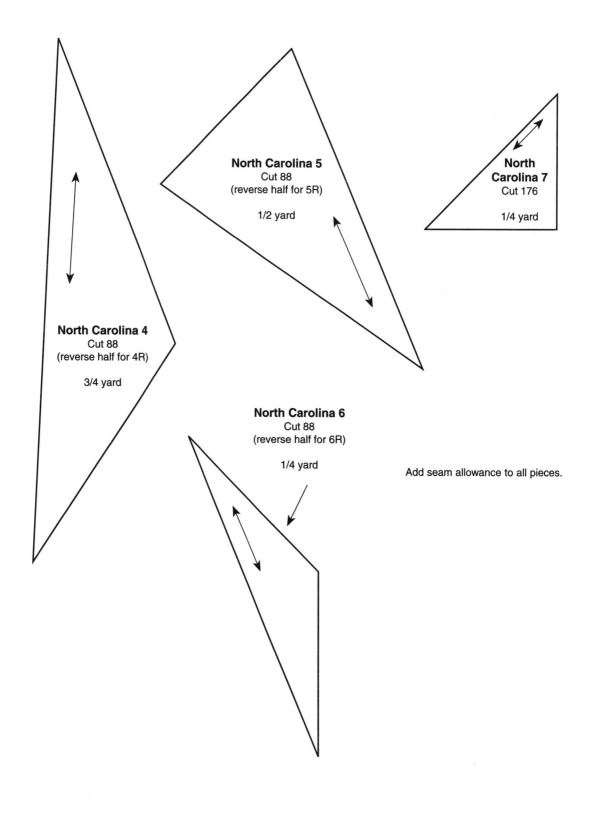

North Carolina 5
Cut 88
(reverse half for 5R)

1/2 yard

North Carolina 7
Cut 176

1/4 yard

North Carolina 4
Cut 88
(reverse half for 4R)

3/4 yard

North Carolina 6
Cut 88
(reverse half for 6R)

1/4 yard

Add seam allowance to all pieces.

North Dakota Pieced Border

You have many color choices to make if you use this pieced border on your quilt center. Using earth-tone colors gives this design a Southwestern flavor.

Border Unit 1: Irregular shape; 9" wide—6 per side
Border Unit 2: Irregular shape; 9" wide—3 per side
Border Unit 3: Irregular shape; 9" wide—2 per side
Corner Unit: Irregular shape; 9" wide—4 corners

> Border is shown with the star pattern for Royal Star of North Dakota. The pattern for the star is available in *Royal Stars of the States*, also published by House of White Birches. See ordering information on Page 159.

North Dakota Pieced Border
Placement Diagram
Star Center 75" x 75"
Add 1 1/2" borders—78" x 78"
With Borders 96" x 96"

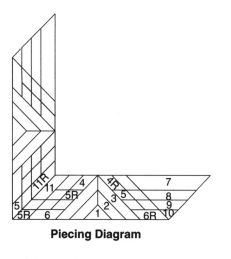

Piecing Diagram

Figure 1
Piece Border Unit 1 as shown. You will
need 6 of these units per side (reverse 3).

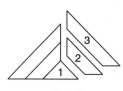

Figure 2
Piece Border Unit 2 as shown. You
will need 3 of these units per side.

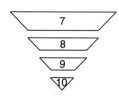

Figure 3
Piece Border Unit 3 as
shown. You will need 2 of
these units per side.

Figure 4
Piece 8 corner units as shown
(reverse half).

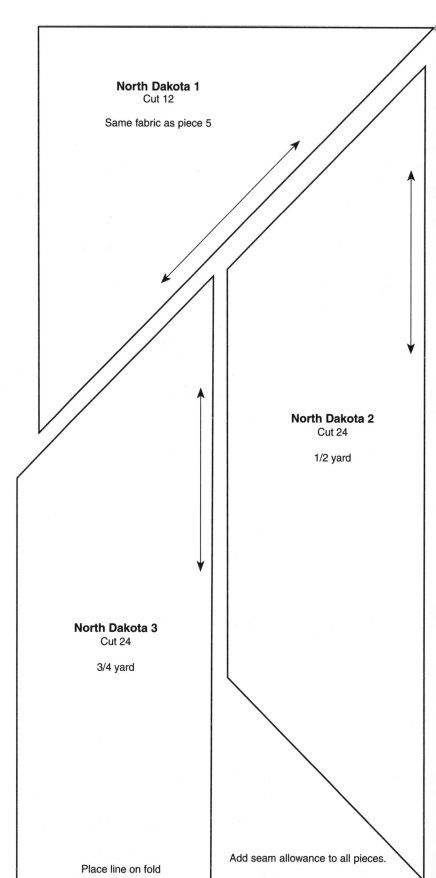

North Dakota 1
Cut 12

Same fabric as piece 5

North Dakota 2
Cut 24

1/2 yard

North Dakota 3
Cut 24

3/4 yard

Place line on fold

Add seam allowance to all pieces.

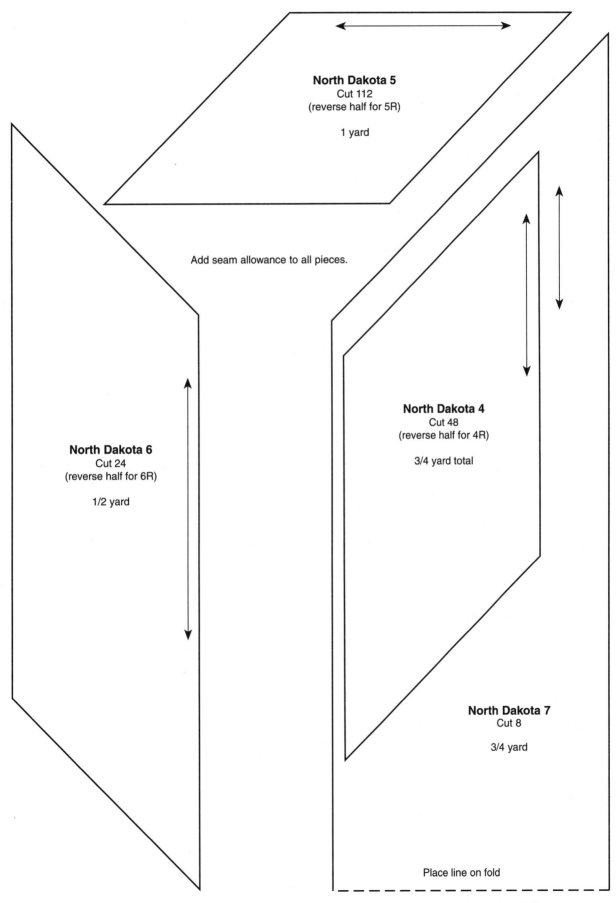

Place line on fold

North Dakota 5
Cut 112
(reverse half for 5R)

1 yard

Add seam allowance to all pieces.

North Dakota 4
Cut 48
(reverse half for 4R)

3/4 yard total

North Dakota 6
Cut 24
(reverse half for 6R)

1/2 yard

North Dakota 7
Cut 8

3/4 yard

Place line on fold

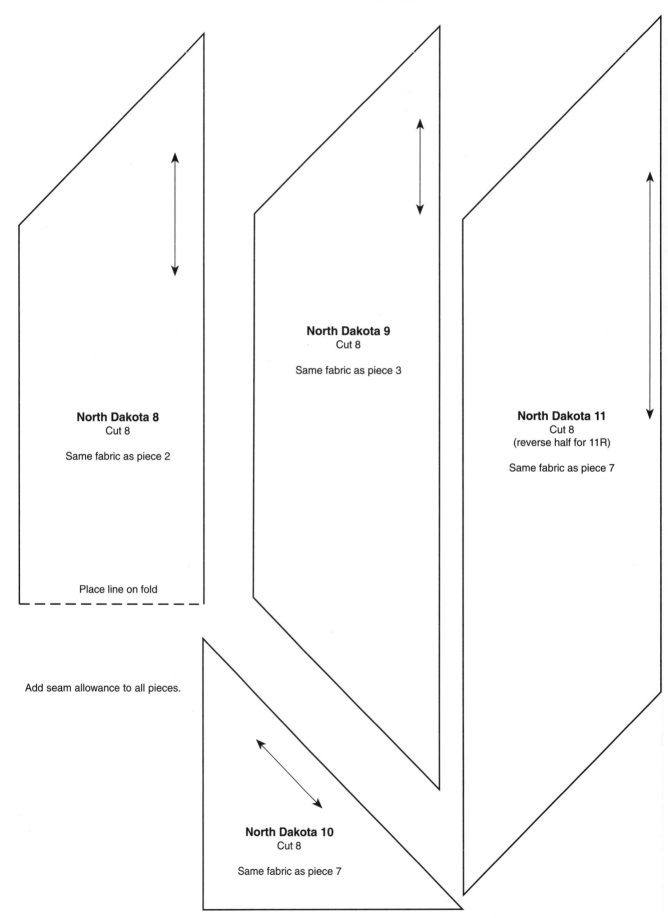

North Dakota 8
Cut 8

Same fabric as piece 2

North Dakota 9
Cut 8

Same fabric as piece 3

North Dakota 11
Cut 8
(reverse half for 11R)

Same fabric as piece 7

North Dakota 10
Cut 8

Same fabric as piece 7

Place line on fold

Add seam allowance to all pieces.

Ohio Pieced Border

The points on the Ohio pieced border look like Indian arrowheads. If you prefer them to point outward, reverse the direction of the units before stitching to your quilt center to observe the effect.

Border Unit: 7 1/2" x 8"—10 per side
Corner Unit: 8" x 8"—4 corners

Border is shown with the star pattern for Royal Star of Ohio. The pattern for the star is available in *Royal Stars of the States*, also published by House of White Birches. See ordering information on Page 159.

Ohio Pieced Border
Placement Diagram
75" x 75"
With Borders 91" x 91"

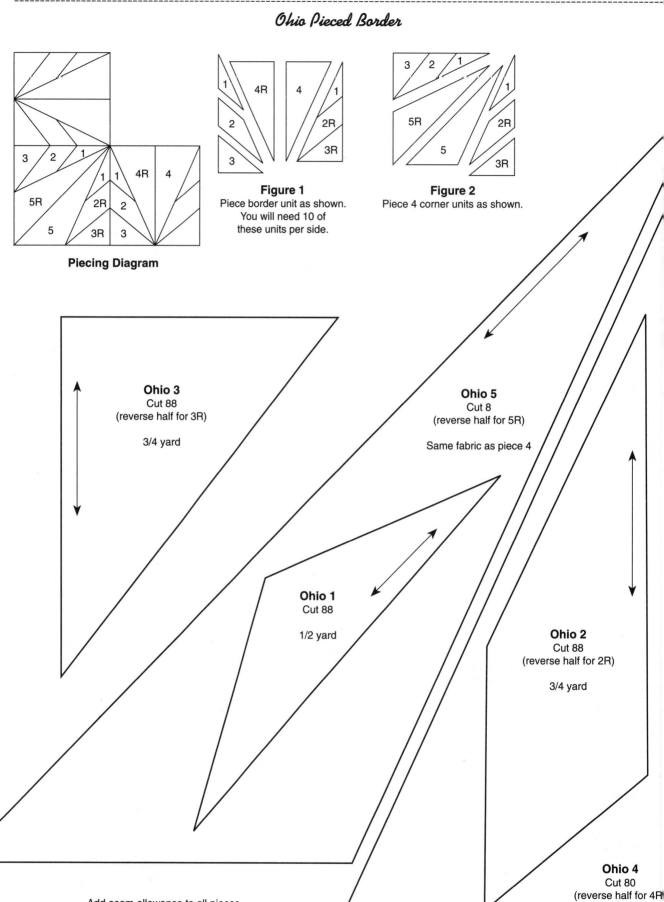

Piecing Diagram

Figure 1
Piece border unit as shown.
You will need 10 of
these units per side.

Figure 2
Piece 4 corner units as shown.

Ohio 3
Cut 88
(reverse half for 3R)

3/4 yard

Ohio 5
Cut 8
(reverse half for 5R)

Same fabric as piece 4

Ohio 1
Cut 88

1/2 yard

Ohio 2
Cut 88
(reverse half for 2R)

3/4 yard

Ohio 4
Cut 80
(reverse half for 4R)

1 1/2 yards

Add seam allowance to all pieces.

Oklahoma Pieced Border

Here is yet another simple diamond-shape border pattern. Two pattern pieces make up the side units with only two more pieces in the corners. Add this easy border to any quilt with diamond shapes in the center.

Border Unit: Irregular shape; 5" wide—39 per side
Corner Unit: Irregular shape; 5" wide—4 corners

Border is shown with the star pattern for Royal Star of Oklahoma. The pattern for the star is available in *Royal Stars of the States*, also published by House of White Birches. See ordering information on Page 159.

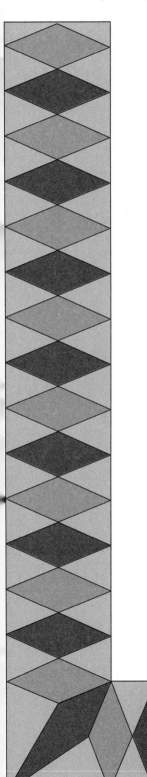

Oklahoma Pieced Border
Placement Diagram
Star Center 77" x 77"
Add 1 1/2" borders—80" x 80"
With Borders 90" x 90"

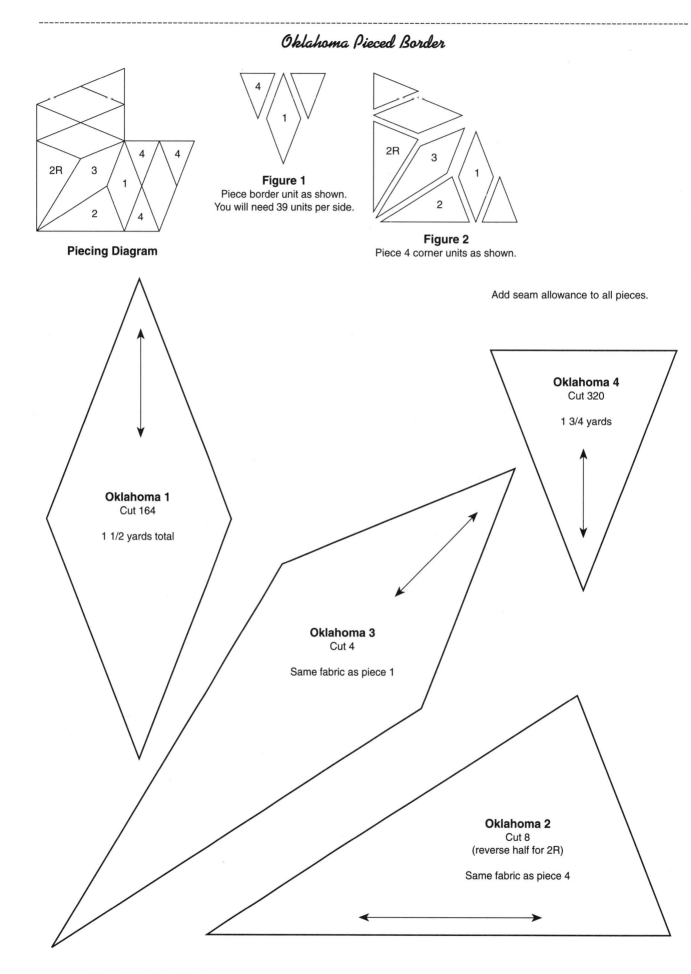

Figure 1
Piece border unit as shown.
You will need 39 units per side.

Piecing Diagram

Figure 2
Piece 4 corner units as shown.

Add seam allowance to all pieces.

Oklahoma 1
Cut 164

1 1/2 yards total

Oklahoma 3
Cut 4

Same fabric as piece 1

Oklahoma 4
Cut 320

1 3/4 yards

Oklahoma 2
Cut 8
(reverse half for 2R)

Same fabric as piece 4

Oregon Pieced Border

Although this border looks complicated, it really works up easily, even by machine. You don't have to confess to those who admire your quilt how easy it was—accept the compliments with grace and chuckle as you keep your secret.

Border Unit: 5" x 8"—15 per side
Corner Unit: 8" x 8"—4 corners

Border is shown with the star pattern for Royal Star of Oregon. The pattern for the star is available in *Royal Stars of the States*, also published by House of White Birches. See ordering information on Page 159.

Oregon Pieced Border
Placement Diagram
Star Center 75" x 75"
With Borders 91" x 91"

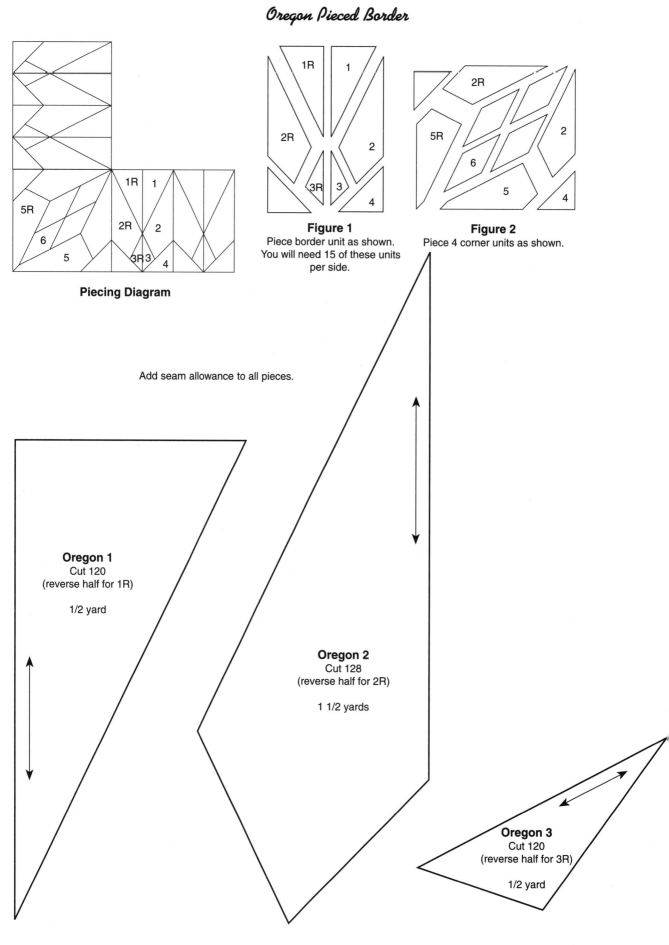

Piecing Diagram

Figure 1
Piece border unit as shown.
You will need 15 of these units
per side.

Figure 2
Piece 4 corner units as shown.

Add seam allowance to all pieces.

Oregon 1
Cut 120
(reverse half for 1R)

1/2 yard

Oregon 2
Cut 128
(reverse half for 2R)

1 1/2 yards

Oregon 3
Cut 120
(reverse half for 3R)

1/2 yard

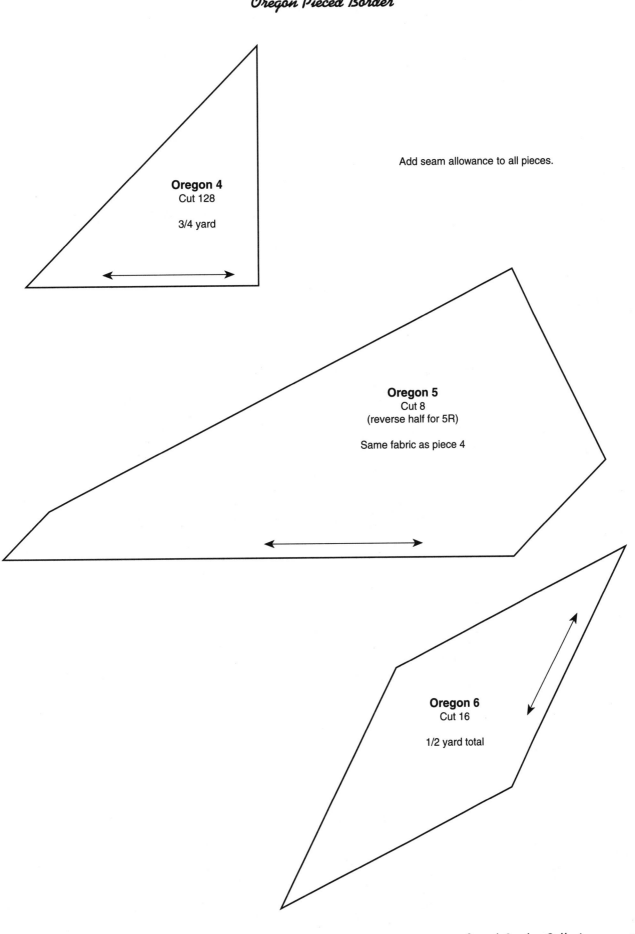

Add seam allowance to all pieces.

Oregon 4
Cut 128

3/4 yard

Oregon 5
Cut 8
(reverse half for 5R)

Same fabric as piece 4

Oregon 6
Cut 16

1/2 yard total

Pennsylvania Pieced Border

The large pieces used to complete this border design make piecing go by fast. The design is balanced by the use of a dark color in piece 3. Repeat colors from the center in the corner stars to create unity.

Border Unit 1: Diamond shape; 8" wide—7 per side
Border Unit 2: Diamond shape; 8" wide—6 per side
Border Unit 3: Irregular shape; 8" wide—2 per side
Corner Unit: 8" x 8" square—4 corners

Border is shown with the star pattern for Royal Star of Pennsylvania. The pattern for the star is available in *Royal Stars of the States*, also published by House of White Birches. See ordering information on Page 159.

Pennsylvania Pieced Border
Placement Diagram
Star Center 75" x 75"
With Borders 91" x 91"

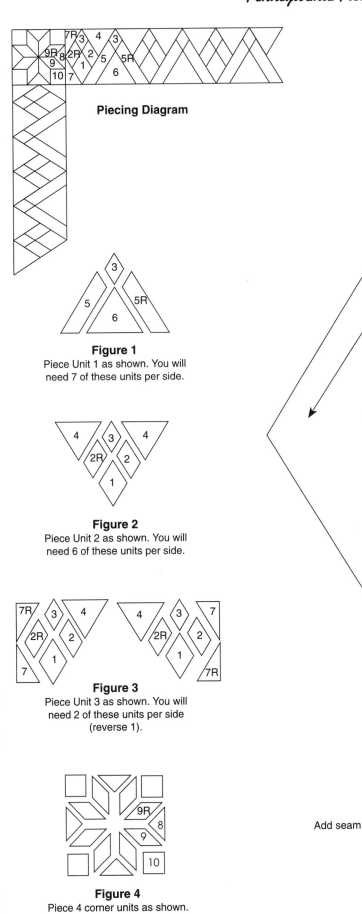

Piecing Diagram

Figure 1
Piece Unit 1 as shown. You will
need 7 of these units per side.

Figure 2
Piece Unit 2 as shown. You will
need 6 of these units per side.

Figure 3
Piece Unit 3 as shown. You will
need 2 of these units per side
(reverse 1).

Figure 4
Piece 4 corner units as shown.

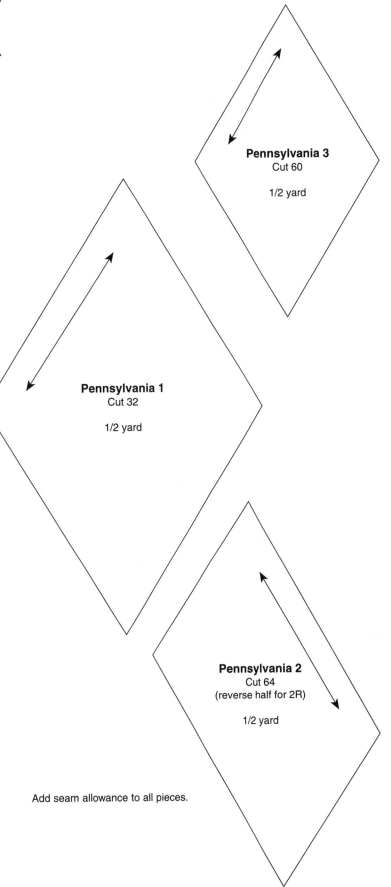

Pennsylvania 3
Cut 60

1/2 yard

Pennsylvania 1
Cut 32

1/2 yard

Pennsylvania 2
Cut 64
(reverse half for 2R)

1/2 yard

Add seam allowance to all pieces.

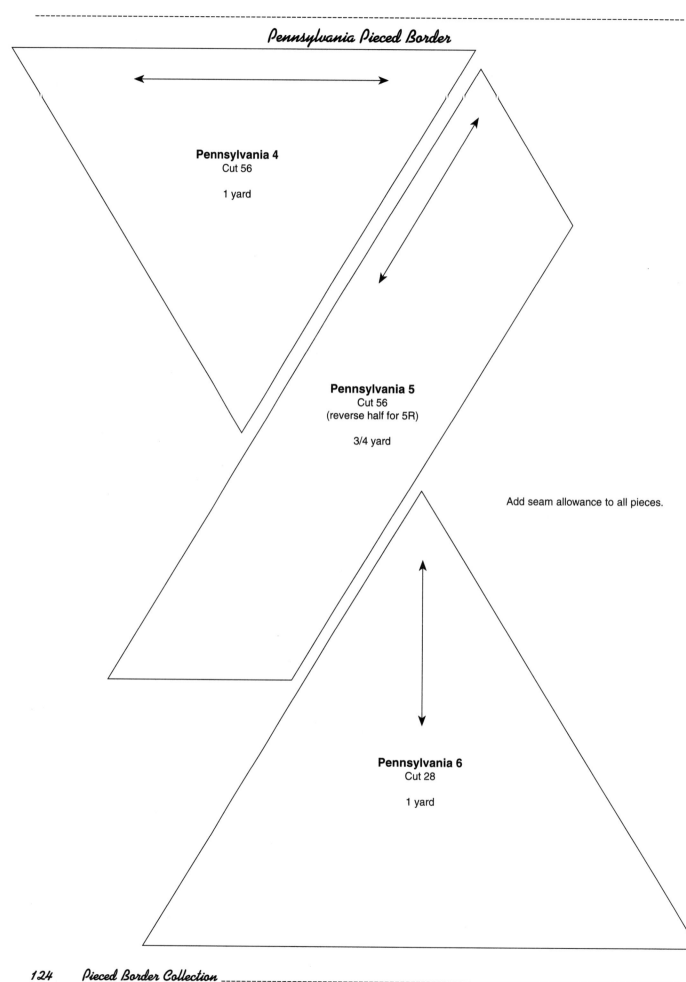

Pennsylvania 4
Cut 56

1 yard

Pennsylvania 5
Cut 56
(reverse half for 5R)

3/4 yard

Add seam allowance to all pieces.

Pennsylvania 6
Cut 28

1 yard

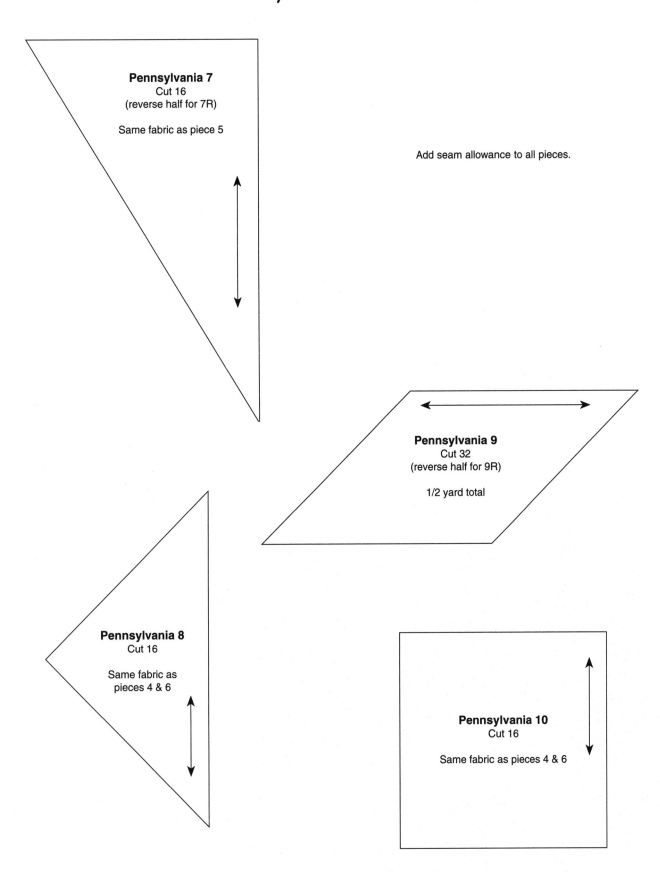

Pennsylvania 7
Cut 16
(reverse half for 7R)

Same fabric as piece 5

Add seam allowance to all pieces.

Pennsylvania 9
Cut 32
(reverse half for 9R)

1/2 yard total

Pennsylvania 8
Cut 16

Same fabric as
pieces 4 & 6

Pennsylvania 10
Cut 16

Same fabric as pieces 4 & 6

Rhode Island Pieced Border

If you like to strip-piece your borders, this design is for you. Cut fabric strips for pieces 1, 2 and 3 at least 70" long by 2 1/8" wide (plus seams) and join together. Cut at angles and sew to the piece 1 units to fit your quilt center.

Border Unit 1: Irregular shape; 6 3/8" wide—2 per side
Border Unit 2: Irregular shape; 6 3/8" wide—1 per side

Border is shown with the star pattern for Royal Star of Rhode Island. The pattern for the star is available in *Royal Stars of the States*, also published by House of White Birches. See ordering information on Page 159.

Rhode Island Pieced Border
Placement Diagram
Star Center 75" x 75"
With Borders 87 3/4" x 87 3/4"

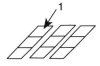

Figure 1
Piece Border Unit 1 as shown. You will
need 2 of these units per side.

Figure 2
Piece Border Unit 2 as shown. You will
need 1 of these units per side.

Piecing Diagram

Add seam allowance to all pieces.

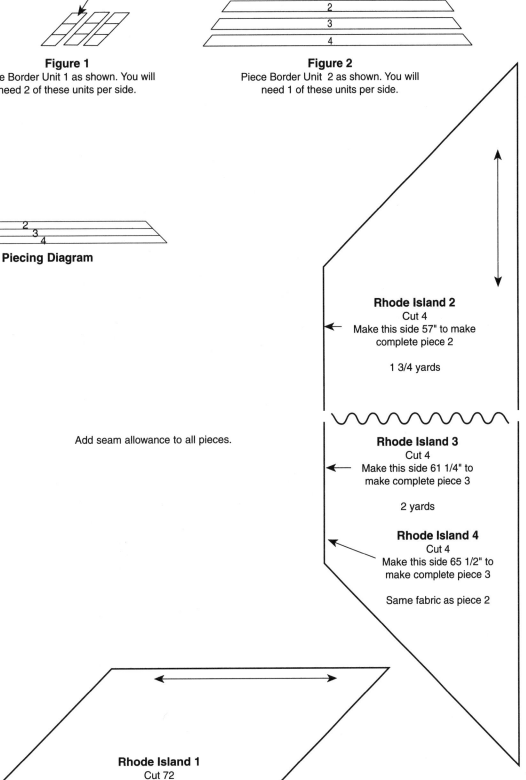

Rhode Island 2
Cut 4
Make this side 57" to make
complete piece 2

1 3/4 yards

Rhode Island 3
Cut 4
Make this side 61 1/4" to
make complete piece 3

2 yards

Rhode Island 4
Cut 4
Make this side 65 1/2" to
make complete piece 3

Same fabric as piece 2

Rhode Island 1
Cut 72

1/2 yard total

South Carolina Pieced Border

If you would like to be a bit creative, use only one of the two border units used in the South Carolina design to make a totally different-looking border. It is easy to personalize any one of the designs in this book by combining them with units of the same width from another border. Have fun playing with this one.

Border Unit 1: 8" x 8"—4 per side
Border Unit 2: 8" x 8"—4 per side
Border Unit 3: 4" x 8"—2 per side
Corner Unit: 8" x 8"—4 corners

Border is shown with the star pattern for Royal Star of South Carolina. The pattern for the star is available in *Royal Stars of the States*, also published by House of White Birches. See ordering information on Page 159.

South Carolina Pieced Border
Placement Diagram
Star Center 72" x 72"
With Borders 88" x 88"

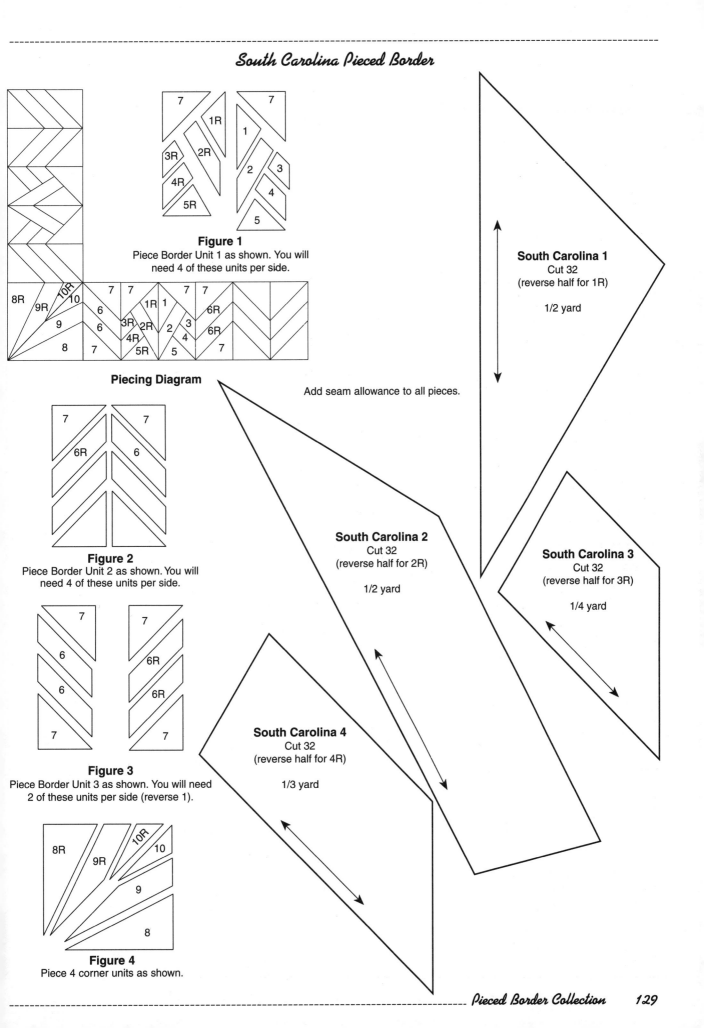

Figure 1
Piece Border Unit 1 as shown. You will
need 4 of these units per side.

Piecing Diagram

Add seam allowance to all pieces.

Figure 2
Piece Border Unit 2 as shown. You will
need 4 of these units per side.

Figure 3
Piece Border Unit 3 as shown. You will need
2 of these units per side (reverse 1).

Figure 4
Piece 4 corner units as shown.

South Carolina 1
Cut 32
(reverse half for 1R)

1/2 yard

South Carolina 2
Cut 32
(reverse half for 2R)

1/2 yard

South Carolina 3
Cut 32
(reverse half for 3R)

1/4 yard

South Carolina 4
Cut 32
(reverse half for 4R)

1/3 yard

Add seam allowance to all pieces.

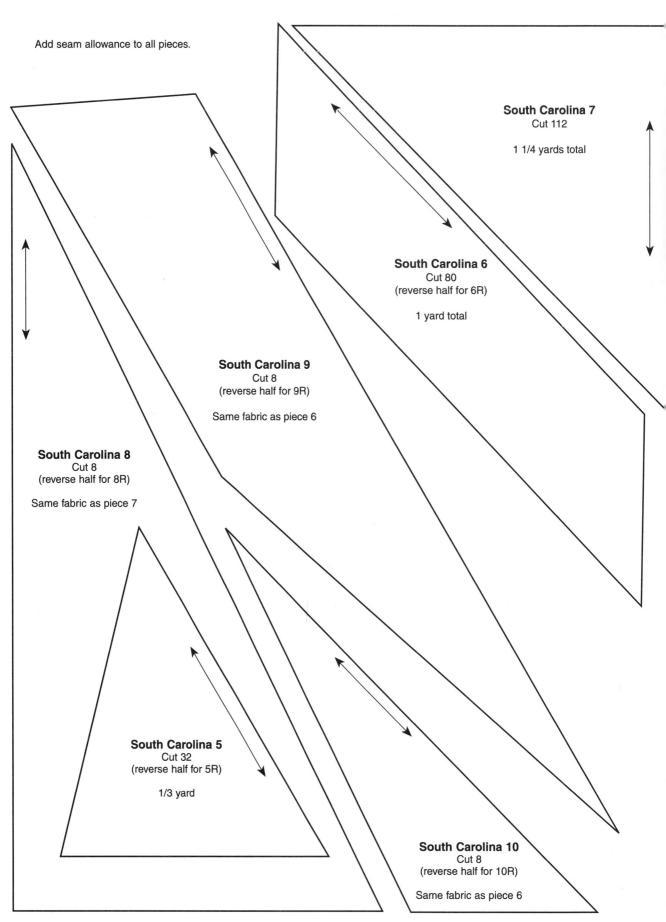

South Carolina 7
Cut 112

1 1/4 yards total

South Carolina 6
Cut 80
(reverse half for 6R)

1 yard total

South Carolina 9
Cut 8
(reverse half for 9R)

Same fabric as piece 6

South Carolina 8
Cut 8
(reverse half for 8R)

Same fabric as piece 7

South Carolina 5
Cut 32
(reverse half for 5R)

1/3 yard

South Carolina 10
Cut 8
(reverse half for 10R)

Same fabric as piece 6

South Dakota Pieced Border

Add this border to your quilt center accurately and you will take a prize when you enter the quilt in a competition. Hand-piecing is recommended, even for the experienced machine piecer!

Border Unit 1: Irregular shape; 8" wide—9 per side
Border Unit 2: Irregular shape; 8" wide—8 per side
Border Unit 3: Irregular shape; 8" wide—2 per side
Corner Unit: Irregular shape; 8" wide—4 corners

Border is shown with the star pattern for Royal Star of South Dakota. The pattern for the star is available in *Royal Stars of the States*, also published by House of White Birches. See ordering information on Page 159.

South Dakota Pieced Border
Placement Diagram
Star Center 75" x 75"
Add 1" borders—77" x 77"
With Borders 93" x 93"

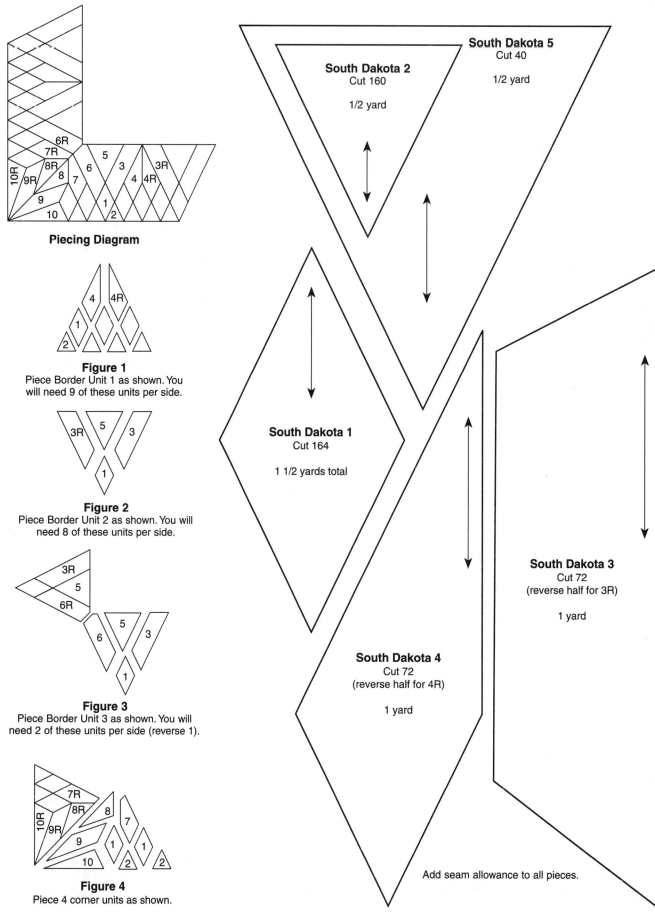

Piecing Diagram

Figure 1
Piece Border Unit 1 as shown. You
will need 9 of these units per side.

Figure 2
Piece Border Unit 2 as shown. You will
need 8 of these units per side.

Figure 3
Piece Border Unit 3 as shown. You will
need 2 of these units per side (reverse 1).

Figure 4
Piece 4 corner units as shown.

South Dakota 5
Cut 40

1/2 yard

South Dakota 2
Cut 160

1/2 yard

South Dakota 1
Cut 164

1 1/2 yards total

South Dakota 3
Cut 72
(reverse half for 3R)

1 yard

South Dakota 4
Cut 72
(reverse half for 4R)

1 yard

Add seam allowance to all pieces.

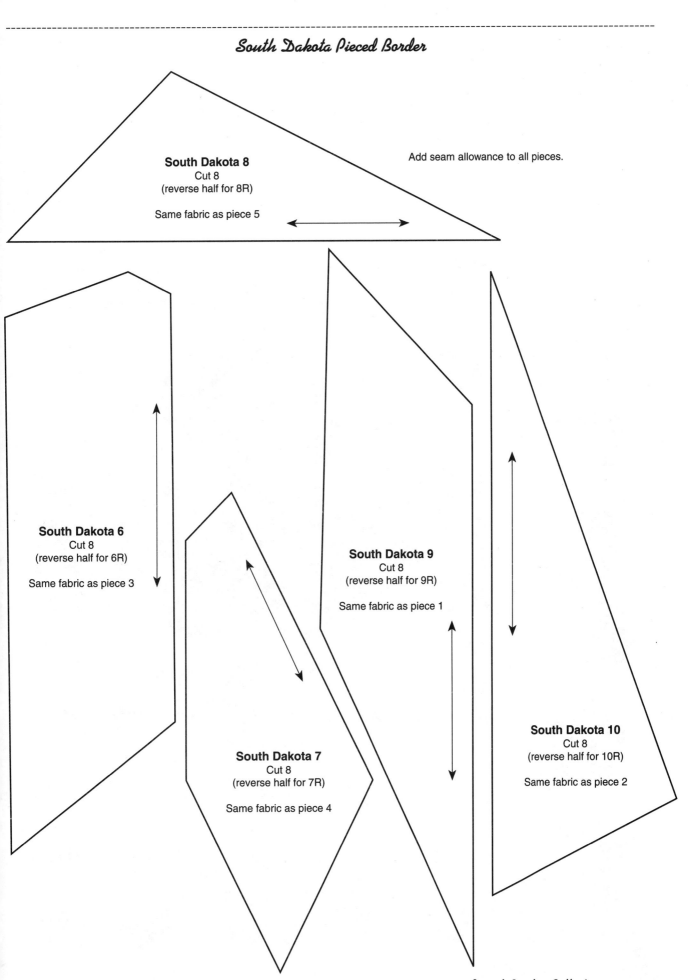

South Dakota 8
Cut 8
(reverse half for 8R)

Same fabric as piece 5

Add seam allowance to all pieces.

South Dakota 6
Cut 8
(reverse half for 6R)

Same fabric as piece 3

South Dakota 9
Cut 8
(reverse half for 9R)

Same fabric as piece 1

South Dakota 7
Cut 8
(reverse half for 7R)

Same fabric as piece 4

South Dakota 10
Cut 8
(reverse half for 10R)

Same fabric as piece 2

Tennessee Pieced Border

Your quilt will make a bold statement when finished with this striking border design. Repeat the colors from your quilt's center to balance the large border pieces with the smaller pieces.

Border Unit: 8" x 9"—10 per side
Corner Unit: 9" x 9"—4 corners needed

Border is shown with the star pattern for Royal Star of Tennessee. The pattern for the star is available in *Royal Stars of the States*, also published by House of White Birches. See ordering information on Page 159.

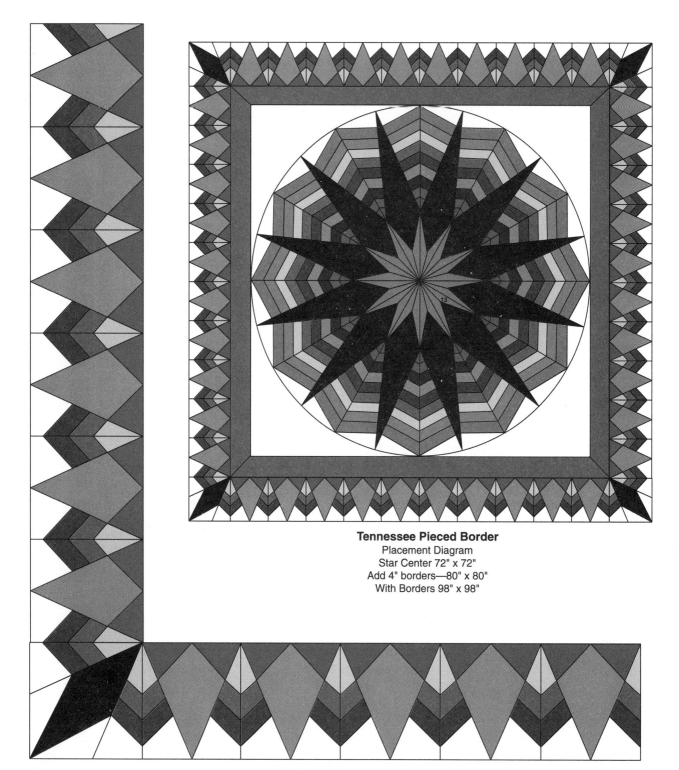

Tennessee Pieced Border
Placement Diagram
Star Center 72" x 72"
Add 4" borders—80" x 80"
With Borders 98" x 98"

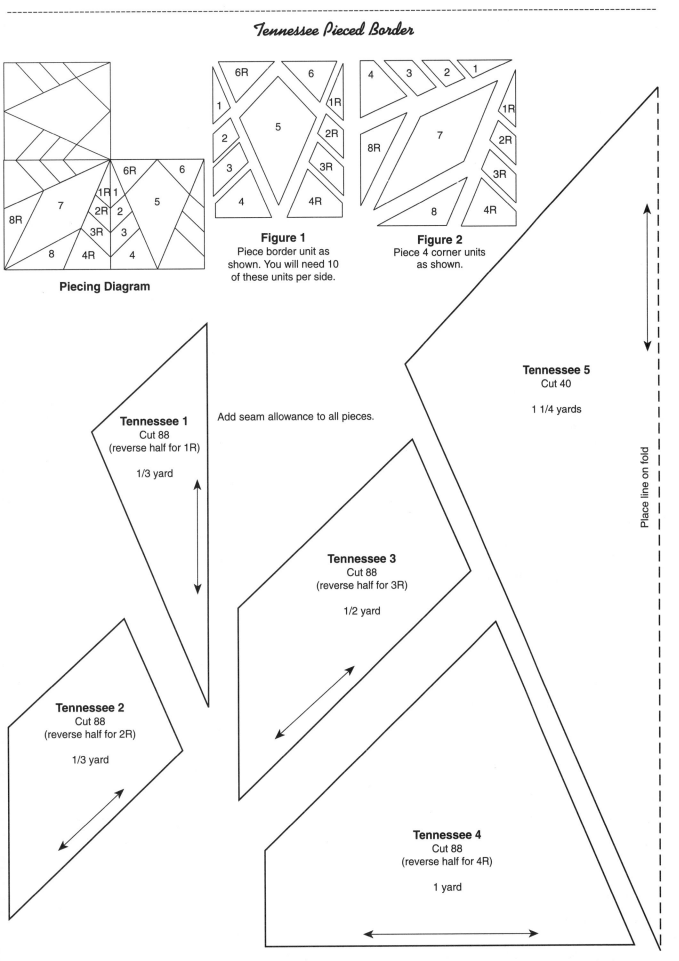

Tennessee Pieced Border

Piecing Diagram

Figure 1
Piece border unit as
shown. You will need 10
of these units per side.

Figure 2
Piece 4 corner units
as shown.

Add seam allowance to all pieces.

Tennessee 1
Cut 88
(reverse half for 1R)

1/3 yard

Tennessee 2
Cut 88
(reverse half for 2R)

1/3 yard

Tennessee 3
Cut 88
(reverse half for 3R)

1/2 yard

Tennessee 4
Cut 88
(reverse half for 4R)

1 yard

Tennessee 5
Cut 40

1 1/4 yards

Place line on fold

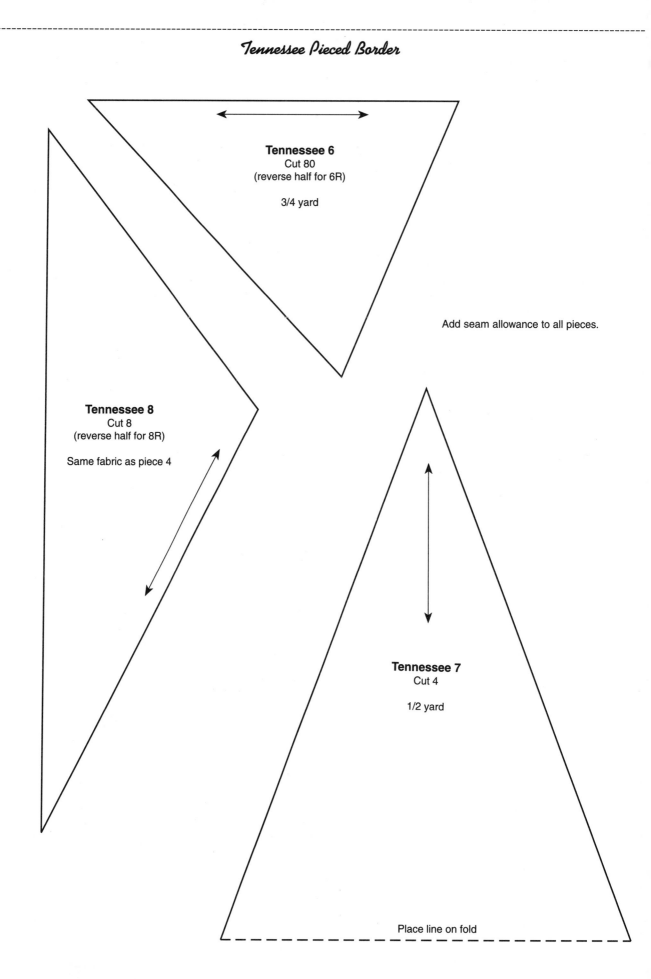

Tennessee 6
Cut 80
(reverse half for 6R)

3/4 yard

Add seam allowance to all pieces.

Tennessee 8
Cut 8
(reverse half for 8R)

Same fabric as piece 4

Tennessee 7
Cut 4

1/2 yard

Place line on fold

Texas Pieced Border

Frame your quilt center with this bold pieced border design. Although complicated-looking, it is not too difficult to construct.

Border Unit 1: Irregular shape; 8" wide—10 per side
Border Unit 2: Irregular shape; 8" wide—9 per side
Corner Unit: Irregular shape; 8" wide—4 corners

Border is shown with the star pattern for Royal Star of Texas. The pattern for the star is available in *Royal Stars of the States*, also published by House of White Birches. See ordering information on Page 159.

Texas Pieced Border
Placement Diagram
Star Center 75" x 75"
Add 2 1/2" borders—80" x 80"
With Borders 96" x 96"

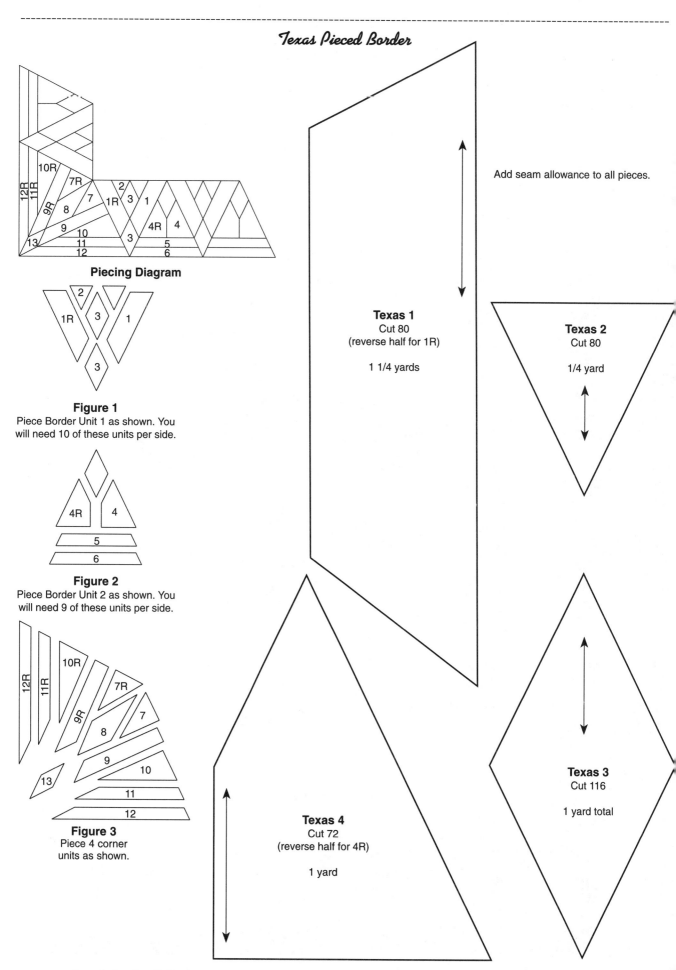

Piecing Diagram

Figure 1
Piece Border Unit 1 as shown. You
will need 10 of these units per side.

Figure 2
Piece Border Unit 2 as shown. You
will need 9 of these units per side.

Figure 3
Piece 4 corner
units as shown.

Add seam allowance to all pieces.

Texas 1
Cut 80
(reverse half for 1R)

1 1/4 yards

Texas 2
Cut 80

1/4 yard

Texas 3
Cut 116

1 yard total

Texas 4
Cut 72
(reverse half for 4R)

1 yard

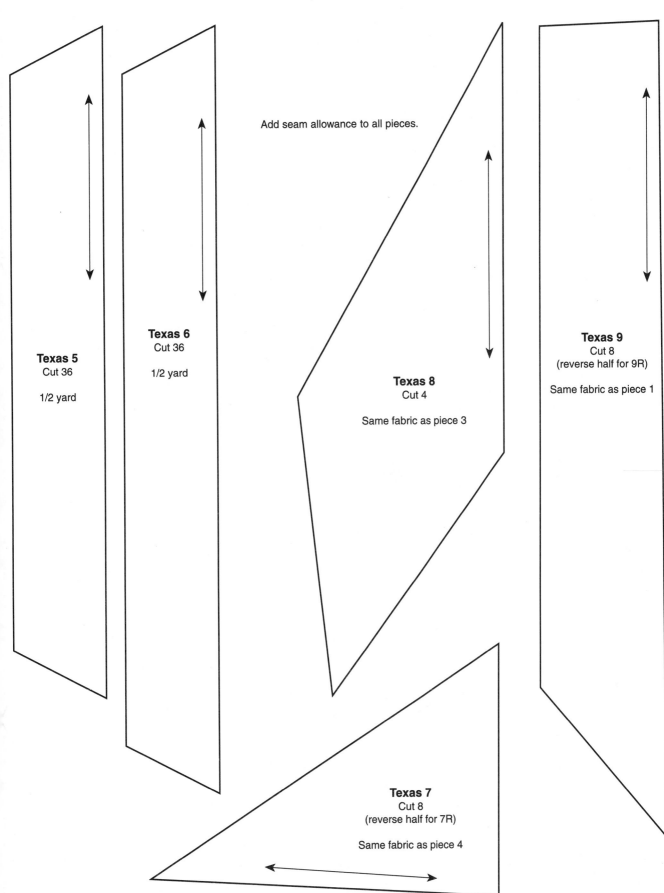

Add seam allowance to all pieces.

Texas 5
Cut 36

1/2 yard

Texas 6
Cut 36

1/2 yard

Texas 8
Cut 4

Same fabric as piece 3

Texas 9
Cut 8
(reverse half for 9R)

Same fabric as piece 1

Texas 7
Cut 8
(reverse half for 7R)

Same fabric as piece 4

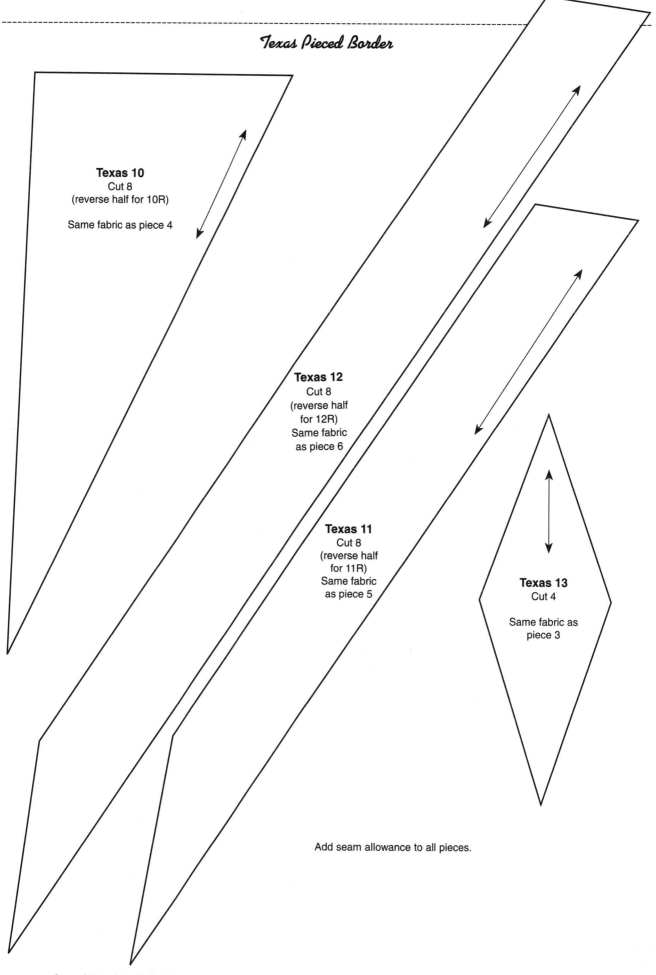

Texas 10
Cut 8
(reverse half for 10R)

Same fabric as piece 4

Texas 12
Cut 8
(reverse half
for 12R)
Same fabric
as piece 6

Texas 11
Cut 8
(reverse half
for 11R)
Same fabric
as piece 5

Texas 13
Cut 4

Same fabric as
piece 3

Add seam allowance to all pieces.

Utah Pieced Border

The Utah border design requires very precise piecing because of the angled points that all come together at the outside edge. Hand-piecing is recommended.

Border Unit 1: 7 1/2" x 8"—8 per side
Border Unit 2: Irregular shape; 8" wide—2 per side
Corner Unit: Irregular shape; 8" wide—4 corners

Border is shown with the star pattern for Royal Star of Utah. The pattern for the star is available in *Royal Stars of the States*, also published by House of White Birches. See ordering information on Page 159.

Utah Pieced Border
Placement Diagram
Star Center 75" x 75"
With Borders 91" x 91"

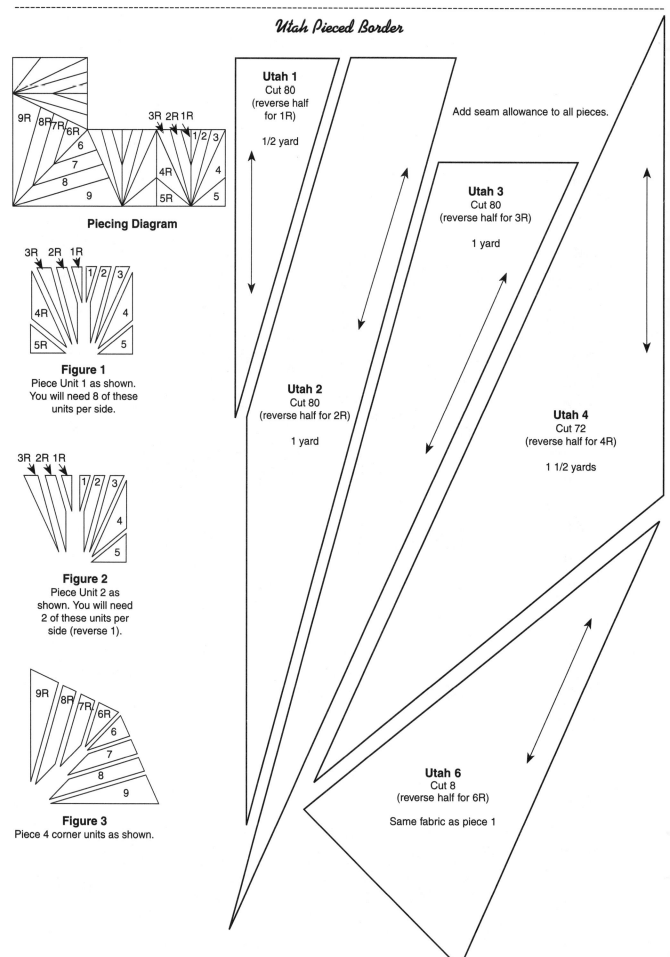

Piecing Diagram

3R 2R 1R

Figure 1
Piece Unit 1 as shown.
You will need 8 of these
units per side.

3R 2R 1R

Figure 2
Piece Unit 2 as
shown. You will need
2 of these units per
side (reverse 1).

9R 8R 7R 6R

Figure 3
Piece 4 corner units as shown.

Utah 1
Cut 80
(reverse half
for 1R)

1/2 yard

Utah 2
Cut 80
(reverse half for 2R)

1 yard

Add seam allowance to all pieces.

Utah 3
Cut 80
(reverse half for 3R)

1 yard

Utah 4
Cut 72
(reverse half for 4R)

1 1/2 yards

Utah 6
Cut 8
(reverse half for 6R)

Same fabric as piece 1

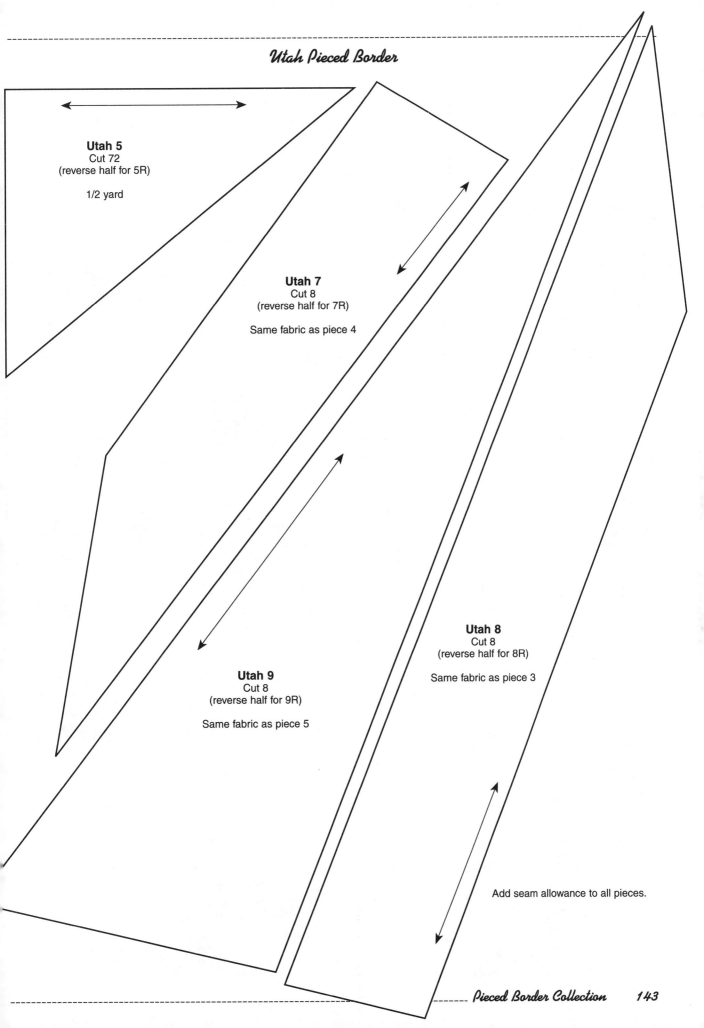

Utah 5
Cut 72
(reverse half for 5R)

1/2 yard

Utah 7
Cut 8
(reverse half for 7R)

Same fabric as piece 4

Utah 9
Cut 8
(reverse half for 9R)

Same fabric as piece 5

Utah 8
Cut 8
(reverse half for 8R)

Same fabric as piece 3

Add seam allowance to all pieces.

Vermont Pieced Border

Any star center would be complemented by this pretty border. Be careful when cutting and sewing piece 1 as it is not the same measurement on all sides and must be reversed. A notch has been added to the longest side. Use the notch as a guide for piecing the proper sides of piece 1 together.

Border Unit: Irregular shape—6" wide

Border is shown with the star pattern for Royal Star of Vermont. The pattern for the star is available in *Royal Stars of the States*, also published by House of White Birches. See ordering information on Page 159.

Vermont Pieced Border
Placement Diagram
Star Center 75" x 75"
Add 1 1/2" borders—78" x 78"
With Borders 90" x 90"

Vermont Pieced Border

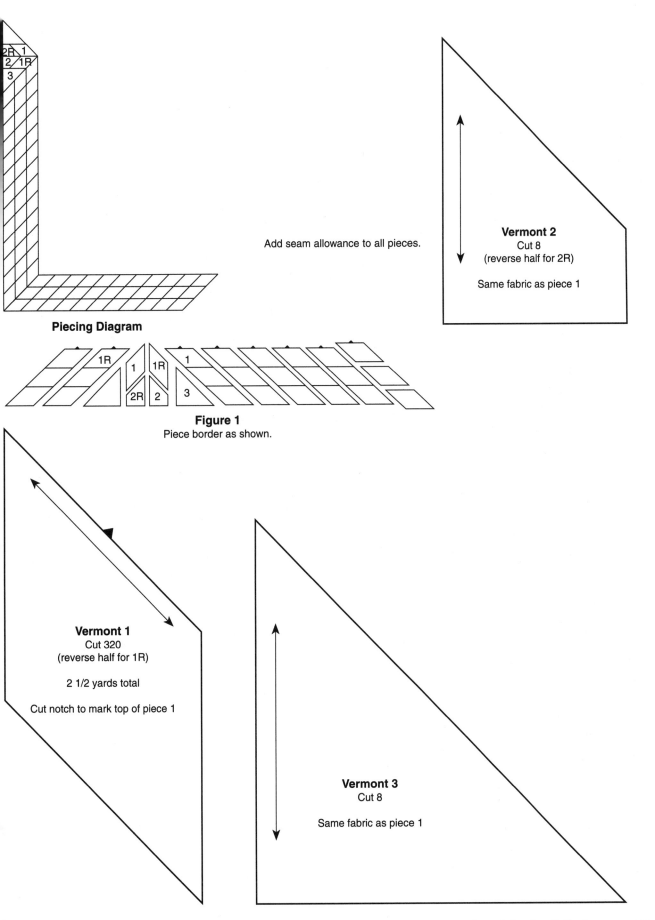

Piecing Diagram

Add seam allowance to all pieces.

Vermont 2
Cut 8
(reverse half for 2R)

Same fabric as piece 1

Figure 1
Piece border as shown.

Vermont 1
Cut 320
(reverse half for 1R)

2 1/2 yards total

Cut notch to mark top of piece 1

Vermont 3
Cut 8

Same fabric as piece 1

Virginia Pieced Border

What a pretty combination the colors and shapes in the Virginia Pieced Border make! The border units are made using large-size pieces, making this an easy border to piece.

Border Unit: 8" x 8"—9 per side
Corner Unit: 8" x 8"—4 corners

Border is shown with the star pattern for Royal Star of Virginia. The pattern for the star is available in *Royal Stars of the States*, also published by House of White Birches. See ordering information on Page 159.

Virginia Pieced Border
Placement Diagram
Star Center 72" x 72"
With Borders 88" x 88"

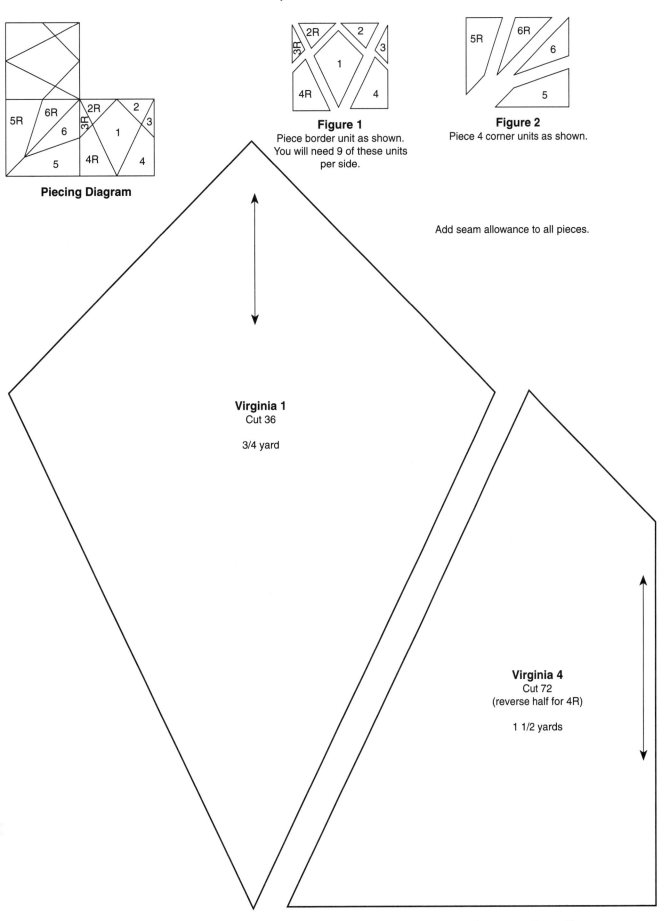

Piecing Diagram

Figure 1
Piece border unit as shown.
You will need 9 of these units
per side.

Figure 2
Piece 4 corner units as shown.

Add seam allowance to all pieces.

Virginia 1
Cut 36

3/4 yard

Virginia 4
Cut 72
(reverse half for 4R)

1 1/2 yards

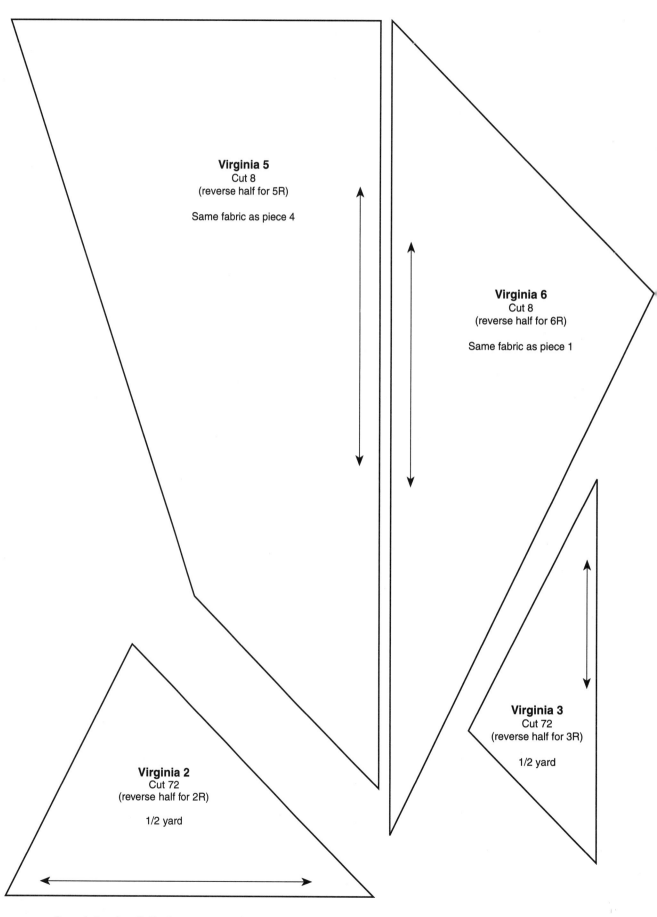

Washington Pieced Border

Use patriotic colors of red, white and blue to make this pretty border. The design is easy to piece and the shapes are well-proportioned. Have fun adding this border to your latest quilt creation!

Border Unit: 6" x 10"—12 per side
Corner Unit: 10" x 10"—4 corners

Border is shown with the star pattern for Royal Star of Washington. The pattern for the star is available in *Royal Stars of the States*, also published by House of White Birches. See ordering information on Page 159.

Washington Pieced Border
Placement Diagram
Star Center 72" x 72"
With Borders 92" x 92"

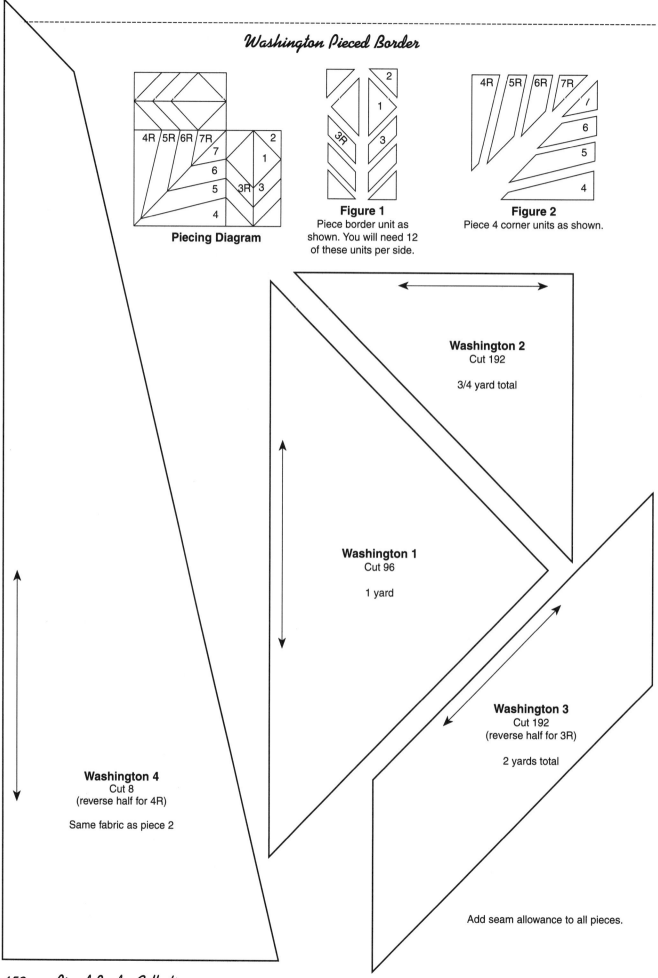

Washington Pieced Border

Piecing Diagram

Figure 1
Piece border unit as shown. You will need 12 of these units per side.

Figure 2
Piece 4 corner units as shown.

Washington 2
Cut 192

3/4 yard total

Washington 1
Cut 96

1 yard

Washington 3
Cut 192
(reverse half for 3R)

2 yards total

Washington 4
Cut 8
(reverse half for 4R)

Same fabric as piece 2

Add seam allowance to all pieces.

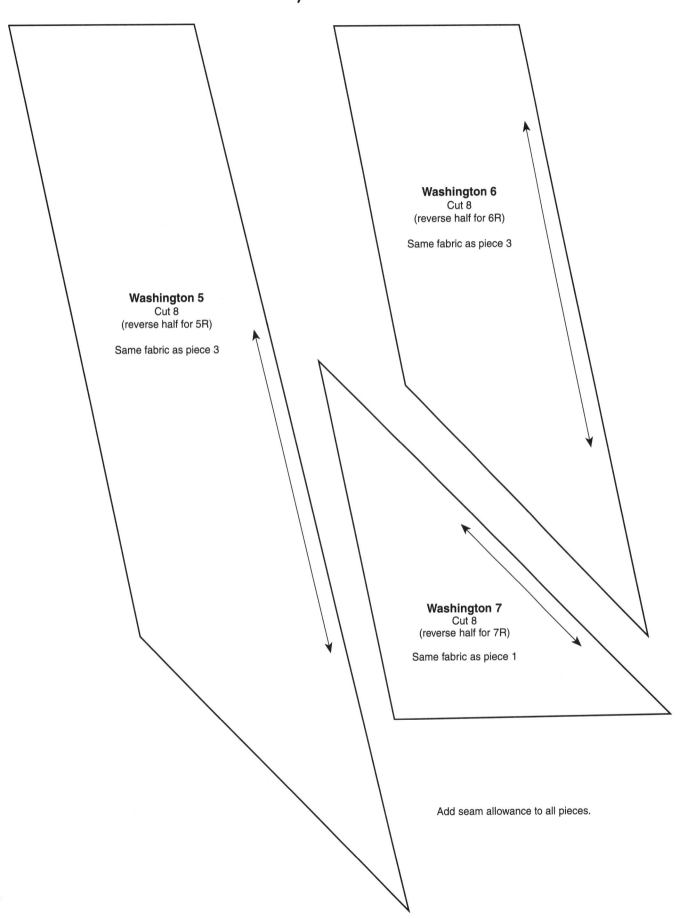

Washington 6
Cut 8
(reverse half for 6R)

Same fabric as piece 3

Washington 5
Cut 8
(reverse half for 5R)

Same fabric as piece 3

Washington 7
Cut 8
(reverse half for 7R)

Same fabric as piece 1

Add seam allowance to all pieces.

West Virginia Pieced Border

An unpieced fabric strip is sewn between the pieced units in this border, making it easy to machine-piece and quick to stitch.

Border Unit: Rectangle; 2" x 4"—40 per side
Corner Unit: 6" x 6"—4 corners

Border is shown with the star pattern for Royal Star of West Virginia. The pattern for the star is available in *Royal Stars of the States*, also published by House of White Birches. See ordering information on Page 159.

West Virginia Pieced Border
Placement Diagram
Star Center 75" x 75"
Add 2 1/2" borders—80" x 80"
With Borders 92" x 92"

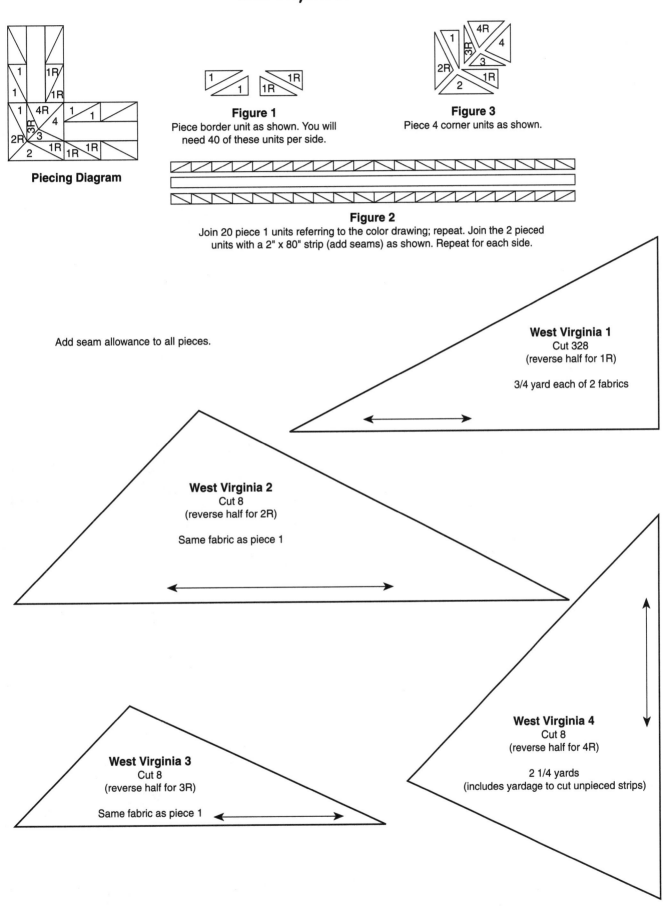

Piecing Diagram

Figure 1
Piece border unit as shown. You will
need 40 of these units per side.

Figure 3
Piece 4 corner units as shown.

Figure 2
Join 20 piece 1 units referring to the color drawing; repeat. Join the 2 pieced
units with a 2" x 80" strip (add seams) as shown. Repeat for each side.

Add seam allowance to all pieces.

West Virginia 1
Cut 328
(reverse half for 1R)

3/4 yard each of 2 fabrics

West Virginia 2
Cut 8
(reverse half for 2R)

Same fabric as piece 1

West Virginia 4
Cut 8
(reverse half for 4R)

2 1/4 yards
(includes yardage to cut unpieced strips)

West Virginia 3
Cut 8
(reverse half for 3R)

Same fabric as piece 1

Wisconsin Pieced Border

You don't always need to choose a complicated border to enhance your quilt center. Adding a narrow border strip to the quilt center and around the outside edge of the pieced border frames the whole design for a clean and simple look.

Border Unit: Irregular shape; 6" wide—27 per side
Corner Unit: Irregular shape; 6" wide—4 corners

Border is shown with the star pattern for Royal Star of Wisconsin. The pattern for the star is available in *Royal Stars of the States*, also published by House of White Birches. See ordering information on Page 159.

Wisconsin Pieced Border
Placement Diagram
Star Center 75" x 75"
Add 1 1/2" borders—78" x 78"
With Borders 93" x 93"

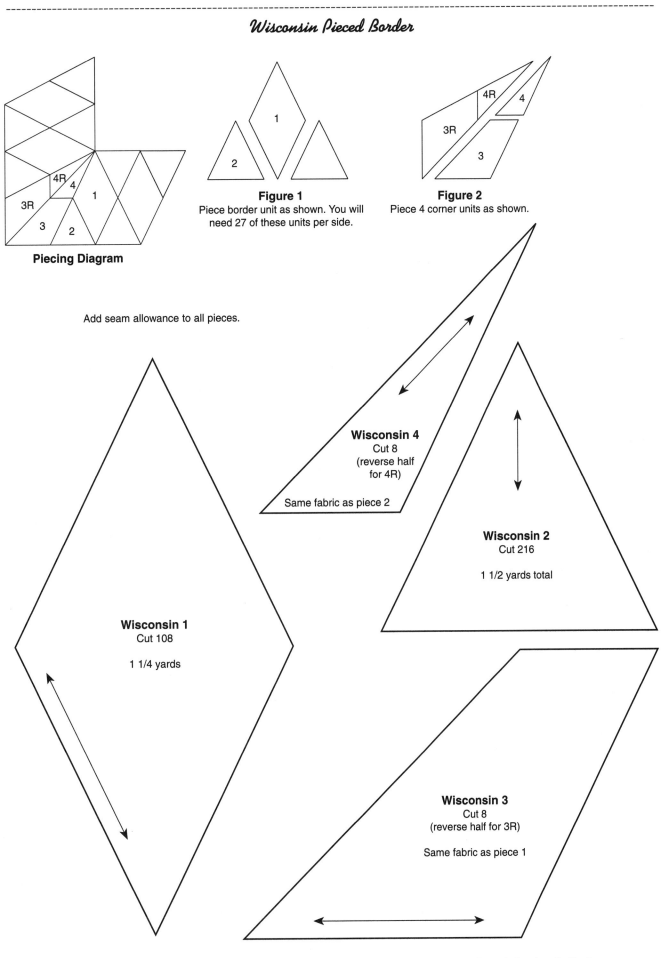

Piecing Diagram

Figure 1
Piece border unit as shown. You will
need 27 of these units per side.

Figure 2
Piece 4 corner units as shown.

Add seam allowance to all pieces.

Wisconsin 4
Cut 8
(reverse half
for 4R)

Same fabric as piece 2

Wisconsin 2
Cut 216

1 1/2 yards total

Wisconsin 1
Cut 108

1 1/4 yards

Wisconsin 3
Cut 8
(reverse half for 3R)

Same fabric as piece 1

Wyoming Pieced Border

Piecing this diamond-shaped border is easy compared to some of the other designs in this book. It can be easily machine-pieced because of the larger pieces.

Border Unit: Irregular shape; 5" wide—15 per side
Corner Unit: Irregular shape; 5" wide—4 corners

Border is shown with the star pattern for Royal Star of Wyoming. The pattern for the star is available in *Royal Stars of the States*, also published by House of White Birches. See ordering information on Page 159.

Wyoming Pieced Border
Placement Diagram
Star Center 75" x 75"
Add 2" borders—79" x 79"
With Borders 93" x 93"

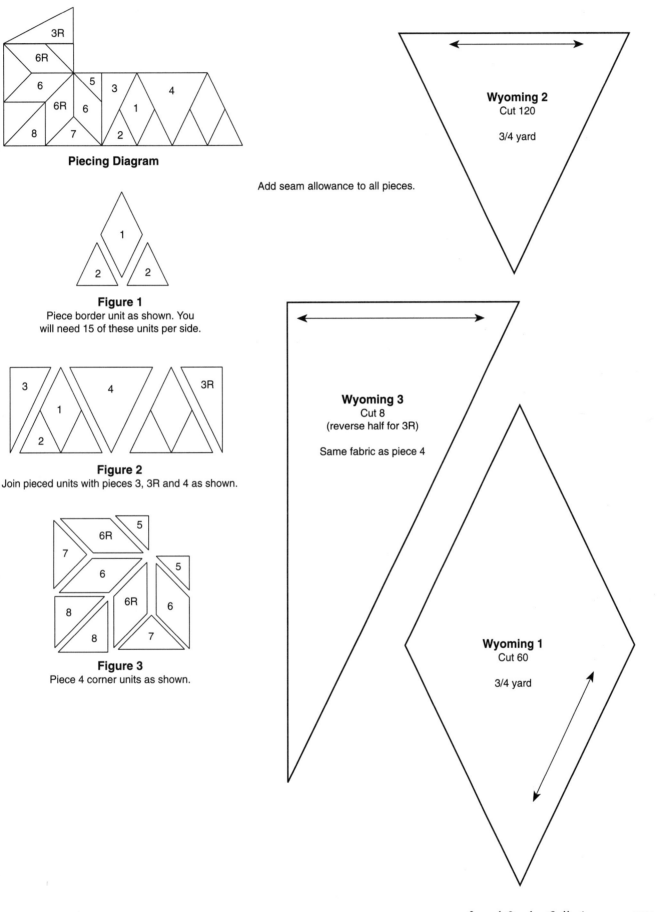

Piecing Diagram

Figure 1
Piece border unit as shown. You
will need 15 of these units per side.

Figure 2
Join pieced units with pieces 3, 3R and 4 as shown.

Figure 3
Piece 4 corner units as shown.

Add seam allowance to all pieces.

Wyoming 2
Cut 120

3/4 yard

Wyoming 3
Cut 8
(reverse half for 3R)

Same fabric as piece 4

Wyoming 1
Cut 60

3/4 yard

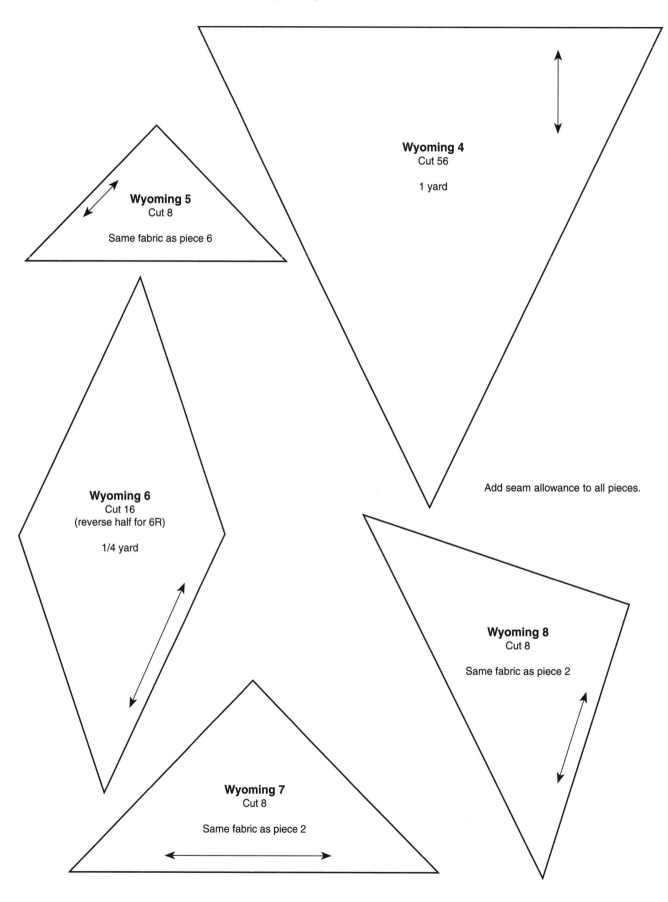

Wyoming 4
Cut 56

1 yard

Wyoming 5
Cut 8

Same fabric as piece 6

Wyoming 6
Cut 16
(reverse half for 6R)

1/4 yard

Add seam allowance to all pieces.

Wyoming 8
Cut 8

Same fabric as piece 2

Wyoming 7
Cut 8

Same fabric as piece 2

Royal Stars OF THE STATES

50 Majestic Quilts
You can make!

You may be wondering ...

... about the vibrant star quilts you see pictured with the border patterns in this copy of *Pieced Border Collection*. They demonstrate how those beautiful pieced borders work with finished quilts.

Well, all 50 star quilt patterns (plus several more borders) are available to you in a full-size companion volume called *Royal Stars of the States*. And, we would like to send you a copy for a *free* 21-day inspection! There's no obligation to buy and no need to send any money now!

You're sure to be interested in this unique book filled with a total of 50—yes, 50!—star quilt patterns. Each one is dedicated to one of the states in our great country!

Royal Stars of the States features complete, easy-to-follow instructions and detailed diagrams to guide you as you make these color-filled and exquisitely designed collector quilts.

Send for your no-risk preview copy today!

**Coordinated Border Patterns!
Detailed Diagrams!**

HOUSE of WHITE BIRCHES

Royal Stars

OF THE STATES
50 MAJESTIC QUILTS WITH COMPLETE INSTRUCTIONS

Stars Galore!
Fast, Easy Instructions

How to Order:
Simply send in the postage-paid order card attached to the reverse side of this page to receive **Royal Stars of the States** for a free 21-day inspection. If you decide to keep the book you'll pay in three easy installments of $4.99 (plus shipping and handling).

There's no need to send money now! And, if you're not completely satisfied you are free to return **Royal Stars of the States**—no questions asked. If the card on the reverse side is missing simply write to this address:

Royal Stars of the States, P.O. Box 9001, Big Sandy, Texas 75755

Order your companion volume today!